ALSO BY ROSE NAFTALIN

*Grandma Rose's Book
of Sinfully Delicious
Cakes, Cookies,
Pies, Cheese Cakes,
Cake Rolls & Pastries*

GRANDMA ROSE'S BOOK OF SINFULLY DELICIOUS SNACKS, NIBBLES, NOSHES & OTHER DELIGHTS

RANDOM HOUSE
NEW YORK

GRANDMA ROSE'S BOOK OF SINFULLY DELICIOUS SNACKS, NIBBLES, NOSHES & OTHER DELIGHTS

ROSE NAFTALIN

This book is dedicated to:

MY CHILDREN

MY GRANDCHILDREN

MY GREAT-GRANDCHILDREN

Library of Congress Cataloging in Publication Data
Naftalin, Rose.
    Grandma Rose's Book of sinfully delicious snacks,
nibbles, noshes & other delights.
    Includes index.
    1. Snack foods. 2. Cookery (Appetizers)
3. Desserts. I. Title. II. Title: Book of sinfully
delicious snacks, nibbles, noshes & other delights.
TX740.N33 1978   641.5'3   78-57130
ISBN 0-394-42733-5

BOOK DESIGN AND ILLUSTRATIONS
BY LILLY LANGOTSKY

Manufactured in the United States of America
4 6 8 9 7 5 3

FOREWORD

This is a book of nibbles. Some are sweets . . . candies, prepared fruits, tarts and cakes. Some are fish or meat or vegetable "finger food," the kind you'd serve at a party or give to your family as a special treat. A few of the dishes would be a little messy if you tried to manage them with your fingers but they are prepared in bite-size pieces and can be eaten only with a fork, plate perched on your lap, or if necessary, while you're standing at a cocktail party.

On the last three recipes of the book I've cheated: they are full-scale, large, serious desserts, included here only because so many people have asked me for the recipes, I didn't feel I could write a book without them—even if they don't exactly fit the concept.

As many of you know, I started seriously studying how to cook and bake when, as a young bride, I realized that I had married a man who loved fine food and that I knew nothing about how to prepare it. Then, during the Depression, when we, like so many other Americans, fell upon hard times, my husband and I opened a little delicatessen in Toledo, Ohio. We worked round the clock, boiling corned beef on the one-burner stove in the store, setting the yeast dough to rise in our apartment at one in the morning. Yet, after my husband died, it was my skill in cooking that allowed me to raise two small children and then to educate them.

Eventually we all settled in Portland, Oregon, where my restaurant "Rose's" became quite famous. The recipes in this book as well as in my first book come out of this long life of cooking and baking to please my family, my friends, my customers and—now—my readers.

ACKNOWLEDGMENTS

My deepest thanks to Random House, especially to dear Charlotte Mayerson, my editor, who had faith and confidence and proved such an inspiration to me.

To Bonnie, my daughter-in-law, who has worked hard and conscientiously typing all the recipes, and to Davida, my daughter, for her efforts and endless patience in checking all my work—my loving thanks.

This book was made possible by the support of my family and friends. I want you to know how grateful I feel for all of your help.

You, the public, have overwhelmed me with your enthusiastic acceptance of my efforts and response to my first book, *Grandma Rose's Book of Sinfully Delicious Cakes, Cookies, Pies, Cheese Cakes, Cake Rolls & Pastries*. Please accept my sincere thanks.

Above all, writing this book has been such a joy. I could almost taste the things I was writing about. My family and friends had a wonderful time feasting on the tested results.

January 1978

Rose Naftalin

CONTENTS

VEGETABLES

ARTICHOKE WITH PÂTÉ

These can be served freshly made, or made ahead of time and chilled until ready to use.

1 14-ounce can artichoke bottoms	4 large mushrooms, coarsely chopped
1 tablespoon butter	Salt and pepper
½ pound fresh chicken livers	Pinch of thyme
1 small onion, finely chopped	1 tablespoon brandy
	1 egg yolk, hard-cooked and sieved

Drain the artichoke bottoms.

Melt the butter in a skillet, add the livers, onion, mushrooms, salt and pepper, and thyme. Sauté for about 10 minutes. The livers should remain a little pink inside. Carefully heat the brandy, pour over the livers and ignite.

Transfer the contents of the skillet to a blender or food processor and whirl until smooth. Spoon a generous amount of pâté on top of each artichoke bottom. Garnish with egg yolk.

COCKTAIL CELERIES

These celery sticks are irresistible and they have almost no calories. Use on an assorted vegetable platter or as a garnish.

If you like to prepare homemade food as gifts, pack these celery sticks neatly in prepared small jars, adding liquid to fill. Seal and store under refrigeration.

1 large bunch celery, unblemished	*1 teaspoon ground fennel seed*
1½ cups water	*1 teaspoon thyme*
Juice of 1 lemon	*1 small bay leaf*
2 tablespoons white vinegar	*1 teaspoon salt*
3 cloves garlic, finely minced	*8 peppercorns, crushed*
½ teaspoon rosemary	*¾ teaspoon coriander, ground*
	1 teaspoon celery salt
	2 large tomatoes, peeled and chopped

Wash and separate the celery stalks. Use vegetable peeler to remove threads of the coarse outside ribs.

Depending on the size, split the ribs lengthwise and cut into thin cocktail sticks 3" or 4" long.

Combine all the ingredients, except the celery, in a large saucepan. Bring to a boil. Add the celery sticks. When the mixture returns to a boil, reduce the heat, cover and cook for 5 minutes.

Spoon the cooked celery into a bowl. Strain the cooking liquid over it. Chill until ready to serve. The celery will keep up to 3 weeks under proper refrigeration.

STUFFED CELERY HEARTS

3 ounces cream cheese,
   at room temperature
1 ounce Roquefort cheese,
   at room temperature

Heart-of-celery stalks
Paprika

Cream the cheeses until smooth. Put the mixture into a pastry bag with a large star tip and fill each celery rib. Cut to desired fingerlength.
   Sprinkle with paprika. Serve as garnish with other appetizers.

FARMERS CHOP SUEY

This very refreshing salad is a traditional summer lunch as well as a nice party dish.

1 small bunch green
   onions, finely chopped
1 cup red radishes,
   thinly sliced
1 cup cucumbers, peeled
   and diced

4 fresh tomatoes, cut in
   chunks
1 small head of lettuce,
   cut in bite size
Salt and pepper to taste
1½ pints sour cream

In a large bowl, combine all the vegetables. Season to taste. Fold in the sour cream. Serve well chilled.

STUFFED CUCUMBERS

This recipe is a little different. We love it.

3 thick cucumbers	Salt and pepper to taste
1 tablespoon salt	½ cup parsley, minced
4 tablespoons butter	2 tablespoons bread crumbs
½ cup onion, minced	½ pint small fresh shucked
½ pound fresh mushrooms,	oysters
finely chopped	3 tablespoons sharp cheese,
Juice of 1 lemon	grated
2 teaspoons tomato paste	Greens for garnish

Peel, cut in half and seed the cucumbers. Scoop out well to give room for the filling. In a large saucepan half filled with water, add salt and bring to a boil. Add the cucumbers and blanch for 5 minutes. Remove from the water and drain.

In a skillet, sauté the onions in butter until golden. Add the mushrooms, lemon juice, tomato paste, salt and pepper. Cook until the liquid is evaporated. Remove from the heat. Add the parsley and bread crumbs. Blend well.

Fill the cavities of the cucumbers. Place a row of oysters on top of each filled cucumber. Sprinkle with the grated cheese. Broil until the cheese is melted.

6

Cut each cucumber half into 4 chunks so you have 24 bite-size pieces. Place on a tray with garnish of greens.

FRENCH-FRIED VEGETABLES

These are popular at parties and yet they are good and nutritious.

BATTER:

1 cup flour	*3 eggs, separated*
1 teaspoon salt	*½ teaspoon olive oil*
½ teaspoon sugar	*½ cup beer*
1 teaspoon dill weed	*2 tablespoons water*

In a bowl, combine the flour, salt, sugar and dill weed. Make a well in the dry ingredients. Add the egg yolks and liquids. Blend well. Beat the egg whites until stiff, then fold into the batter.

VEGETABLES:

2 8-ounce cans artichoke	*3 large zucchini, in 1" slices*
hearts, drained and	*Flour*
sliced in half	*Salt*
1 large head cauliflower,	
in bite-size buds	

7

Preheat oil for deep frying to 375°. Coat the vegetables with flour and shake off excess. Dip the vegetable pieces in the batter and fry until golden brown. Drain on unglazed brown paper. Salt gently.

MARINATED MUSHROOM CAPS

1 pound large fresh mushrooms	*Pinch of thyme*
Juice of 1 lemon	*2 shallots, finely diced*
1 cup tarragon vinegar	*Salt and pepper*
1 clove garlic	*¼ cup olive oil*
1 bay leaf	*1 tablespoon ketchup*
	1 tablespoon dill weed

Wash the mushrooms and remove the stems. Blanch the mushroom caps for 5 minutes in a little salted water to which the lemon juice has been added. Drain and dry.

Combine the vinegar, garlic, bay leaf, thyme, shallots, salt and pepper. Cook for 5 minutes. Cool. Remove the garlic clove. Add the oil and ketchup. Immerse the mushroom caps in the mixture and marinate for 3 hours in the refrigerator.

To serve, drain the mushrooms and place them in a bowl. Sprinkle with dill weed.

MUSHROOM TARTS

These are so good that my daughter and I get hungry just writing down the recipe.

CRUST:

2 cups flour

1 teaspoon salt

12 tablespoons butter, cold

4 tablespoons ice water

Preheat oven to 400°. Combine the flour and salt. With your fingertips, rub in the butter until the mixture is crumbly. Slowly add the water, cutting it in with a knife or heavy spatula, until a ball is formed.

Moisten a small area of your counter and cover it with waxed paper; sprinkle it lightly with flour. Pinch off little pieces of dough. Roll out to ¼" thickness. Cut with a 3" round cookie cutter and place on back of a 2"-muffin pan, over bottom of each little cup. Press firmly around cup.

Bake for about 10 minutes, or until light-brown. Cool slightly and remove shells from pan. Makes 24 tarts.

FILLING:

7 tablespoons butter

3 medium onions, diced

2 pounds fresh
   mushrooms, chopped

Juice of 1 lemon

2 cups heavy cream

Salt and pepper

2 tablespoons cornstarch

½ cup Gruyère cheese, grated

Melt 3 tablespoons of the butter in a large skillet. Sauté the onions until golden. Add the mushrooms, lemon juice and remaining butter. Cover and cook for 5 minutes. Set aside.

In a saucepan, bring the cream to a low boil. Season with salt and pepper. Blend the cornstarch with a little water and add it slowly to the cream. Keep stirring until thickened. Taste for seasoning, then add to the mushroom mixture.

Fill the tart shells. Sprinkle the tops with the grated cheese. Brown under the broiler before serving.

MUSHROOM TARTS #2

This is another mushroom filling that is very good in a Cream-Cheese Tart Shell (page 181).

5 tablespoons onion,	*4 tablespoons flour*
minced	*1 cup light cream*
½ cup butter	*2 tablespoons parsley, chopped;*
1½ pounds fresh mushrooms,	*extra sprigs for garnish*
finely chopped	*Salt and pepper*
3 tablespoons lemon juice	

In a large skillet, sauté the onions in the butter. Add the mushrooms, sprinkle with lemon juice and cook for about 5 minutes. Blend in the flour. Gradually stir in the cream. Add the parsley, and season to taste. Cook over low heat until thickened.

Fill baked tart shells. Garnish with parsley sprigs.

STUFFED MUSHROOMS WITH ANCHOVY

24 large fresh mushrooms
7 tablespoons butter
Juice of 1 lemon
2 tablespoons shallots,
    chopped
2 cloves garlic, minced

½ cup bread crumbs
1 egg, beaten
2 tablespoons dry vermouth
1 tablespoon parsley, chopped
24 rolled anchovy fillets

Wash the mushrooms. Remove the stems and mince them. Sauté the mushroom caps in 3 tablespoons of the butter. Sprinkle with the lemon juice. Set aside.

Sauté the shallots in 3 tablespoons of the butter. Add the garlic and minced stems; cook for 5 minutes. Stir in the bread crumbs, egg, vermouth and parsley. Cook 2 minutes more.

Stuff the mushroom caps with the cooked mixture. Dot with the remaining butter. Heat under the broiler. When ready to serve, garnish each cap with an anchovy.

OLIVE NUT BALLS

*¼ cup sweet butter, at
room temperature
3 ounces cream cheese,
at room temperature
3 ounces Roquefort or
blue cheese, at
room temperature
2 tablespoons shallots,
finely chopped*

*1 tablespoon brandy
¼ teaspoon dry mustard
Salt and pepper to taste
24 pimento-stuffed green
olives
1 cup walnut or pecan
nutmeats, lightly toasted
and chopped*

Combine the butter, cheeses, shallots, brandy, mustard, and salt and pepper.
Blend well. Chill the mixture for 30 minutes.

Dry the olives. Coat them with the cheese mixture, using butter spreader
or small spatula. Roll each covered olive in the chopped nuts. Chill until
serving time.

ALMOND OLIVE BALLS

These very simple olive balls are also very good. They can be made ahead of
time and refrigerated.

1 small jar of pimento-
   stuffed green olives
3 ounces cream cheese,
   at room temperature

6 tablespoons blanched
   almonds, chopped and
   toasted

Dry the olives. With a small knife, spread the cream cheese on the olives. Roll in the chopped nuts. Serve in paper candy cups.

ONION RINGS

A nice nosh with a cocktail, or just as a nibble.

4 large white onions
2 cups milk
1 cup flour

3 eggs, beaten
1 cup bread crumbs

Preheat deep fat for frying to 375°. Peel the onions and cut into ¼″ slices. Let soak in the milk for 1 hour. When ready to use, lift the rings from the milk. Shake them in the flour. Dip the rings in the beaten eggs, then coat them with the bread crumbs. Prepare all the rings.

In the preheated oil, drop in a few rings at a time and fry until golden brown. Place on paper towels to absorb excess grease. Sprinkle with salt and enjoy them!

POTATO SALAD EN GELÉE

4 pounds potatoes
Aspic
1 bunch celery, sliced
  slantwise
1 bunch green onions,
  bulbs and greens,
  finely chopped
6 hard-cooked eggs,
  chopped

¼ cup parsley, minced
1½ cups mayonnaise
Salt and pepper to taste
Black olives
Pimento
Sprigs of parsley

Boil the potatoes in salt water until tender. While they are cooking, prepare the aspic.

Peel the potatoes while they are still warm. Dice to bite size. Add the celery, onions, eggs and parsley. Fold in the mayonnaise. Season to taste.

Pour a few tablespoons of aspic to cover the bottom of an oiled 2-quart mold. Create a design in the aspic with slices of black olives and pimento. Chill until set. Gently fill the mold with the potato salad. Pour the balance of the aspic over the salad. Refrigerate until set.

When ready to serve, unmold on a serving plate. Garnish with parsley.

ASPIC FOR POTATO SALAD:

2 tablespoons gelatin
4 tablespoons cold water
½ cup white vinegar

1 teaspoon salt
1 tablespoon sugar

Mix the gelatin and water. In a small saucepan, heat the vinegar, salt and sugar. Add the gelatin, stir and cook until gelatin is dissolved, for about 5 minutes.

CHEESE-SPINACH SOUFFLÉ ROLL

This vegetable is one of my family's favorites. It is a spectacular dish!

SOUFFLÉ:

9 large eggs, separated
½ cup butter
8 tablespoons flour
Dash of cayenne pepper

1¾ cups light cream
¾ cup sharp Cheddar cheese, grated
¾ cup Parmesan cheese, grated

Preheat oven to 350°. Spray or butter a 15″ x 12″ jelly-roll pan. Line the pan with heavy wax paper and spray again.

In a large skillet, melt the butter. Using a whisk, blend in the flour and pepper. Gradually stir in the cream and cook until thickened. Beat in the cheeses. Gradually add the egg yolks, stirring constantly.

Beat the egg whites and salt until foamy. Add the cream of tartar and continue beating until stiff. Carefully fold into the cheese sauce, one third at a time.

Pour into the prepared pan. Bake for 20 minutes, or until the center, when touched, feels firm. Turn the sheet of soufflé out on a sheet of aluminum foil.

15

SPINACH FILLING:

3 bunches fresh spinach,
   or 3 10-ounce frozen
   packages
4 tablespoons butter
1 medium-size onion,
   finely chopped
2 cups fresh mushrooms,
   sliced

Salt and pepper
2 tablespoons flour
1½ cups sour cream
½ cup sharp Cheddar
   cheese, diced
Paprika

Wash the fresh spinach thoroughly. Cook for 5 minutes in lightly salted water. Remove from the heat, strain off the liquid and chop finely. Put the spinach in a piece of cheesecloth or a tea towel; twist and squeeze until quite dry.

In a large skillet, melt the butter, then add the onion. When golden, add the mushrooms and season to taste. Blend in the flour, and while stirring, add ½ cup of the cream, spinach and cheese. Cook until the cheese is melted.

Spread the soufflé with the spinach filling. Roll up like a jelly roll, starting from the long side. Place on a serving platter. Spread the roll with the remaining sour cream. Sprinkle with paprika. If necessary, heat up the roll in a 350° oven. To serve: Slice as you would a jelly roll.

SPICED VEGETABLES

Make these a few days ahead of party time, or just have on hand for salad garnish or a low-calorie snack.

4 large carrots, pared	*1 tablespoon salt*
1 large celery heart	*3 cups water*
1 head cauliflower	*½ cup white wine vinegar*
½ pound fresh	*1 tablespoon mixed pickling*
mushrooms	*spices*
½ pound pea pods	*2 teaspoons whole dill seeds*
4 cloves garlic, sliced	*1 teaspoon mustard seeds*

Cut the carrots and celery into 3″ sticks. Break the cauliflower into small flowerets. Clean the mushrooms. Blanch the pea pods. Put all the vegetables in a bowl with the garlic and salt.

Combine the water, vinegar and seasonings, bring to a boil, then pour over the vegetables. Cool and marinate in the refrigerator for several days, or until well pickled.

To serve: Drain the brine and arrange the vegetables on a platter with a favorite dip. I like to use a Spray of Radishes (page 118) as garnish.

MARINATED RAW VEGETABLES

This perfect appetizer for a large group is especially appreciated by guests who are watching calories.

2 heads cauliflower	½ to ¾ cup sugar
3 green peppers	3 cloves garlic, minced
2 pounds small carrots	1 tablespoon salt
1 bunch celery	1 tablespoon prepared mustard
1 bunch broccoli	2 teaspoons tarragon leaves
2 cucumbers	Pepper to taste
1 pound fresh mushrooms	18 cherry tomatoes
4 zucchini	4 tablespoons chives, minced
½ cup salad oil	1 large solid tomato
½ cup olive oil	1 bunch watercress
½ cup white wine vinegar	

Cut up the first eight vegetables into bite-size pieces.

Combine the salad oil, olive oil and vinegar. Add the sugar, garlic, salt, mustard, tarragon and pepper. Pour the mixture over the vegetables. Cover and chill for at least 12 hours or overnight. Stir occasionally.

To serve: Arrange the whole cherry tomatoes on top and sprinkle with the minced chives. For additional garnish, peel the large tomato continuously round and round, until all the tomato is cut. Wind the peeling around your forefinger, forming a "rose," and place on the bunch of watercress in the center of the vegetable platter. Very realistic and attractive!

CHICKEN
&
MEAT

CHICKEN AND SHRIMP EN BROCHETTE
with dipping sauce

½ cup sherry
1 pound fresh shrimp,
   shelled and deveined
Salt and pepper
3 fryer chicken breasts,
   skinned and boned

2 cloves garlic, minced
3 green peppers, in 2″ squares
6 green onions, in 2″ lengths
2 zucchini, sliced and lightly
   floured
1 tablespoon soy sauce

Sprinkle the sherry over the shrimp. Add a dash of salt and pepper. Put a little oil in a large skillet or wok. Sauté the shrimp quickly. Cook to desired doneness and remove from the pan. Cut the chicken in bite-size pieces and sauté, adding a little more oil if necessary. Cook until tender and remove.

Sauté the garlic, green pepper, green onions and zucchini. Season with soy sauce, salt and pepper. Remove the vegetables when tender.

Fill 7″ skewers, alternating shrimp, chicken and vegetables. Keep warm on a hot tray. Garnish with lemon wedges and parsley.

DIPPING SAUCE:

¾ cup soy sauce
2 tablespoons sherry
1 teaspoon sugar

3 tablespoons green onions,
   finely chopped

Mix all the ingredients. Use as a dip for the Chicken and Shrimp en Brochette.

CHICKEN LOGS

Several hours before serving, or the day before, prepare the cheese filling.

CHEESE FILLING:

½ cup fresh mushrooms, finely chopped	*6 boned and skinned chicken breasts*
2 tablespoons butter	*Flour for dusting*
¼ teaspoon salt	*2 eggs, beaten*
Dash of cayenne pepper	*¾ cup dry fine bread crumbs*
2 tablespoons flour	*Oil for frying*
½ cup light cream	
1¼ cups sharp Cheddar cheese, shredded	

Cook the mushrooms in butter for 5 minutes. Season with the salt and pepper. Blend in the flour and add the cream, stirring until the mixture becomes thick. Stir in the cheese and cook on low heat until it is melted. Put the mixture in a 10″ pie pan, cover and chill until firm.

When ready to use, cut the cheese mixture into 12 portions. Shape into short logs, about 2″ long.

Cut the chicken breasts in half. Place a piece between two sheets of waxed paper. Using a wooden mallet and working from the center out to the edge, pound until the meat is about ¼″ thick. Sprinkle lightly with salt. Repeat with each half breast.

Place a cheese log on each piece of chicken and roll up, tucking in the sides and sealing as tightly as possible. Dust the rolls with flour. Dip in the beaten eggs and then in the bread crumbs. Let chill.

About an hour before serving, remove the logs from the refrigerator. Heat vegetable oil in a large skillet. Brown the logs on all sides quickly. Drain on paper towels.

Place the logs in a shallow baking pan in a 325° oven. Bake for 30 to 45 minutes.

Serve on a warm platter. Garnish as desired.

CHICKEN AND PÂTÉ ROLL

This is a very unusual "nosh." The ingredients in this recipe make it acceptable for an interesting and delicious Passover dish.

DOUGH:

*1 6-ounce package potato
   pancake mix**
¼ cup peanut oil
¼ cup matzo meal

½ teaspoon salt
2 eggs
2 cups water

Preheat oven to 450°. Grease a 14″ x 10″ x 2″ baking pan.

To the pancake mix, add the peanut oil, matzo meal, salt, eggs and water. Blend thoroughly, then let stand until the mixture thickens.

With floured hands, pat the dough to make a ½″-thick rectangle in the pan. You may want to divide the dough and make two smaller rectangles.

* Available at the supermarket.

CHICKEN FILLING:

1 2½-pound fryer,
   quartered
Salt and pepper
1 large onion, sliced
2 carrots, scraped, in
   chunks

½ bunch celery,
   coarsely sliced
1 bunch parsley
1 bay leaf
6 whole allspice

Place the chicken in a pot with all the other ingredients, add cold water to cover and bring to a boil. Cook until the chicken is tender. Remove the chicken, skin and bone it, mince it and mix with:

1 teaspoon onion powder
1 egg

½ cup blanched almonds,
   toasted and chopped

Set this filling aside.

½ pound fresh
   mushrooms, sliced

Sauté the mushrooms in a little butter and set aside.

CHICKEN-LIVER PÂTÉ:

4 ounces raw chicken fat
1 medium onion,
   coarsely chopped
1 small onion, grated

1 pound chicken livers
4 eggs, hard-cooked
Salt and pepper
1 egg for brushing

In a large skillet, put the chicken fat cut in small pieces. Cook until partially rendered. Pour rendered liquid fat into a container.

Add the chopped onion to the balance of fat in the skillet. When the onions are golden, add the livers and sauté them until they are cooked.

Place the contents of skillet into a blender or food processor together with the hard-cooked eggs and 4 tablespoons of rendered chicken fat. Mince. Add the grated onion, and salt and pepper to taste.

To assemble:

Down the center of the long side of the rectangle of dough, place a narrow mound of chicken filling. Spread on a layer of chicken-liver pâté. Put sautéed mushrooms on top of the pâté. Fold the dough over the mound of fillings so that it is completely enclosed. Brush the outside of the roll with a beaten egg.

Bake until golden brown, 10 to 15 minutes, in the preheated oven. Slice in 1"-width pieces to serve.

SWEET-AND-SOUR CHICKEN WINGS

Oil for frying   1 cup cornstarch
3 pounds chicken wings   3 eggs, beaten
Salt

Preheat frying oil to 375°; set oven at 350°. Cut the tips from the wings and disjoint. Wash and dry. Lightly salt. Dip in the cornstarch, shake off excess. Then dip in the beaten eggs, drain excess.

Fry the wings in the oil until golden brown. Drain on paper towels. Place the wings on a flat baking pan and pour the sauce over them. Bake for 30 minutes.

SAUCE:

¼ cup soy sauce
½ cup vinegar
½ cup sugar
3 tablespoons ketchup
1 teaspoon salt

½ teaspoon Accent
½ cup red-currant jelly
Juice of 1 lemon
Parsley, sliced oranges and
    pineapple chunks for garnish

Bring all the ingredients except the garnish to a boil, stirring constantly. Reduce the heat and let simmer for 10 minutes. Garnish the serving platter with parsley, oranges and pineapple chunks.

BRAISED CHICKEN WINGS

Start these on the stove and finish in a 350° oven.

4 pounds chicken wings
4 tablespoons chicken fat
   or oil for browning
1 cup diced onions
1 clove garlic, minced
2 tablespoons tomato paste
3 tablespoons flour

1 cup chicken stock
1 cup red wine
1 bay leaf
Salt and pepper
1 pound whole mushrooms
Parsley and whole gherkins
   for garnish

26

Cut off the wing tips and set aside. In a large skillet, brown the wings in fat. Add the onions and garlic.

When all the wings are golden brown, stir in the tomato paste, then blend in the flour. Stir in the broth (see below) and wine. Add the bay leaf and season to taste. Add the fresh mushrooms. Place in the oven and bake until tender, or simmer uncovered on the stove for about 45 minutes.

Serve the wings and mushrooms on a platter, and garnish with parsley and gherkins.

CHICKEN STOCK (BROTH):

The cut-off wing tips	*1 onion*
2 carrots	*1 tablespoon chicken base*
Tops of bunch of celery	*or 2 bouillon cubes*
Parsley	*3 cups water*

Place all the ingredients in a pot and simmer for 1 hour. Strain. Salt to taste.

SESAME CHICKEN DRUMSTICKS

These are good hot or cold.

1 cup cracker crumbs, fine	*½ teaspoon salt*
⅓ cup sesame seeds,	*20 fryer chicken legs*
toasted	*⅓ cup cream*
1 teaspoon paprika	*½ cup butter*

Preheat oven to 375°. Use a 13″ x 9″ x 2″ baking pan. Combine the crumbs, sesame seeds, paprika and salt. Dip the drumsticks in the cream and then roll them in the crumb mixture.

Melt the butter in the baking pan. Place the chicken legs in the pan, turning once to coat with butter.

Bake for 1 hour, or until tender. Wrap the ends of the drumsticks with colored foil for easy serving.

CHICKEN NUT BALLS

This is an interesting nosh. The balls can be prepared ahead and refrigerated until ready to broil.

1 pound cooked fryer chicken breasts	*⅓ cup shallots*
	2 cloves garlic
1½ cups walnuts or pecans, shelled	*2 tablespoons chicken broth*
	Salt and pepper
½ cup lime or lemon juice	*¾ cup yogurt, plain*

Skin, bone and finely dice chicken breasts.

In a blender, combine the nuts, juice, shallots, garlic, broth, salt and pepper. When smooth, reserve 1 cup of the mixture. To the balance, add the chicken. Chill for 1 hour.

When cold, take heaping teaspoonfuls of the mixture and form into balls. Keep chilled until ready to broil and serve. Broil about 5 inches from the heat, turning until lightly brown.

To the rest of the nut mixture, blend in the yogurt. Use this as a dip when eating the chicken balls.

Yields about 2 dozen balls.

ORIENTAL LEMON CHICKEN

This dish involves a few procedures, but your final product will be delicious. Use bamboo skewers if you can find them.

MARINADE:

2 tablespoons soy sauce

2 tablespoons dry sherry

2 teaspoons sesame oil

2 tablespoons garlic, minced

2 teaspoons gingerroot, chopped

2 3-pound fryer chickens, skinned, boned and cut into bite-size pieces

2 eggs, beaten

1 cup cornstarch

½ cup flour

3 cups peanut oil for frying

Mix all the marinade ingredients together and pour over the chicken pieces. Let stand for 20 minutes. Remove the chicken from the marinade. Dip the pieces in the beaten eggs, then in the combined cornstarch and flour.

Heat the oil in a deep skillet and fry the chicken pieces until lightly golden. Remove them from the skillet. Reheat the oil until smoking. Fry the chicken pieces again until golden brown. Remove from the heat and drain on paper towels. Pour all the oil from the skillet except 1 tablespoon.

SAUCE:

1 tablespoon oil from skillet
¾ cup fresh lemon juice
¾ cup chicken stock
6 tablespoons sugar

2 teaspoons sesame oil
2 tablespoons cornstarch
2 tablespoons water

To the 1 tablespoon of oil left in the skillet, add the lemon juice, stock, sugar, sesame oil and cornstarch that has been mixed with the water. Cook and stir until the mixture thickens.

Lightly toss the chicken pieces in the hot sauce. Remove to a serving platter. Spear with bamboo sticks and enjoy to the utmost.

CHICKEN STOCK:

Chicken bones, skin,
   giblets
1 large onion
1 bay leaf

6 peppercorns
Tops of bunch of celery
2 carrots
Parsley

Using what was left of the chicken in the above recipe, combine with the rest of the ingredients in a pot. Cover with cold water, bring to a boil and cook for 1 hour. Cool and skim off visible fat. Salt to taste. Use as needed and freeze excess broth.

CHICKEN LIVERS WITH BACON

½ pound chicken livers   *Salt and pepper*
  (about 12 livers)   *¼ pound lean bacon, sliced*

Season livers with salt and pepper. Wrap each liver in a half slice of bacon. Fasten with toothpick.
    Broil until bacon is crisp on all sides.

CHICKEN LIVERS WITH MUSHROOMS

A very delicious brunch dish or hot pick-up. I like to preface this dish with Snappy Bloody Marys and Crisp Celery Sticks (page 128).

8 tablespoons butter   *1 tablespoon flour*
5 shallots, sliced   *½ cup madeira*
1½ pounds chicken livers,   *2 tablespoons parsley,*
  cut in half   *chopped*
Salt and pepper
¾ pound fresh button
  mushrooms*

* If not available, slice large mushrooms in thirds.

31

In a large skillet on medium heat, melt 4 tablespoons of the butter. Add the shallots. When golden, add the livers. Sauté until well browned, stirring constantly. Salt and pepper to taste.

Remove the shallots and livers from the skillet and wipe it with a paper towel. Return the skillet to high heat, add the balance of the butter and the mushrooms. Sauté quickly, stirring constantly. When the mushrooms turn slightly brown, reduce the heat and, still stirring, sprinkle the flour over the mushrooms. Add the wine and cook for a few minutes. Return the shallots and livers to the skillet and blend thoroughly. Taste for seasonings.

To serve: Place in chafing dish or serving bowl on a hot tray. Sprinkle with chopped parsley.

Spear with pleasure!

CHICKEN SALAD

In the restaurant, this chicken salad was a big favorite with our clientele.

1 3½-pound fryer,
   split in half
1 large onion, cut in half
1 small bunch celery
2 carrots, cleaned and
   coarsely cut
1 bay leaf
6 peppercorns

Small bunch parsley
Salt
4 eggs, hard-cooked and
   chopped
2 tablespoons chives, minced
1 cup mayonnaise
2 tablespoons sour cream

In a 3-quart pan, place the chicken, onion, celery tops and the outside celery stalks cut in chunks, carrots, bay leaf, peppercorns, parsley and salt. Fill the pot with cold water to cover ingredients. Let come to a boil, reduce the heat and simmer until the chicken is tender.

Remove the chicken and let cool. Strain the broth and save to use as soup, or as desired.

Skin and bone the chicken. Cut the meat into small chunks; do not mince. Add the celery heart, finely diced. Add eggs and chives. Mix the mayonnaise and sour cream, and add to the chicken mixture. Do not add all at once; you may need to use less, as salad should not be too moist. Taste for seasoning.

When using the salad for dotlet filling, chop the chicken a little finer.

MAYONNAISE:

4 egg yolks	*1 tablespoon tarragon vinegar*
Juice of 1 lemon	*1 teaspoon dry mustard*
¾ cup vegetable oil	*Salt and pepper to taste*

In a blender, combine the egg yolks and lemon juice. Beat for 5 minutes. With blender running very, very gradually, add oil, then vinegar, mustard and seasoning.

This will yield 1 pint of mayonnaise. Keeps for a week under refrigeration.

DOTLETS FILLED WITH CHICKEN SALAD

These are easy to eat and a delightful treat.

Follow Choux Paste recipe (page 213) to make batter.

Preheat oven to 425°. Slightly grease a cookie sheet. Drop batter on a cookie sheet by the teaspoonfuls, spacing at least 1" apart. Bake at 425° for 10 minutes. Reduce the heat to 350° and bake for about 15 minutes more. The dotlets should be golden brown and puffed up.

When cool, cut a small top off each puff. Fill with chicken salad. When filled, replace the cap.

Optional: For an added touch, top with a rosette of mayonnaise put through a pastry tube with a small-star opening. Add a dash of paprika.

These puffs may be placed in small paper cups for easier handling.

SPICY SMALL BURGERS

*2 pounds round steak,
  ground*
1 egg, beaten
*1 tablespoon instant
  minced onion*
2 tablespoons cold water
Salt and pepper to taste

*8 large pimento-stuffed
  green olives*
*8 small white onions,
  parboiled*
2 green peppers, in 2" squares
8 cherry tomatoes

Combine the meat, egg, minced onion, water, salt and pepper. Form into small thick patties. Thread 8″ skewers with patty, olive, onion, green pepper and cherry tomato.

BASTING SAUCE:

1 cup ketchup   *1 teaspoon prepared mustard*
1 tablespoon horseradish   *1 medium onion, minced*
1 teaspoon Worcestershire
   sauce

In a saucepan, bring all the ingredients to a rolling boil. Brush each filled skewer generously with the sauce.

Broil about 3 inches from the heat until meat is cooked to desired doneness.

Note: I use oil or a nonstick spray on the broiler rack to avoid sticking.

BEEF TENDERLOIN AND MUSHROOM EN BROCHETTE

1 pound beef tenderloin   *1 teaspoon salt*
¾ pound fresh   *1 teaspoon garlic powder*
   mushrooms, medium   *2 teaspoons sugar*
   size   *Pepper to taste*

Trim all fat from the beef and cut the meat into 2″ chunks. Thread meat and mushrooms alternately on 7″ skewers. Mix the seasonings and sprinkle on the meat and mushrooms. Prepare the marinade.

MARINADE:

5 tablespoons soy sauce   6 tablespoons peanut oil
4 tablespoons sherry

Mix the ingredients and pour over the meat and mushrooms. Grill or broil the filled skewers until the meat is done to your taste. At the medium-rare stage of the meat, the mushrooms will be well cooked.

Arrange the kabobs on a platter. Garnish with toast points if you wish.

GREAT SPEAR-IT COMBINATIONS

Preheat the broiler and oil or spray the pan to avoid sticking.

Use bamboo spears, and to ensure against foods slipping off, put cubes of bread on each end of the skewer before grilling. Remove bread before serving.

After you've filled the spears, marinate them in a combination of ¼ cup soy sauce and juice of 1 lemon, with 2 tablespoons of peanut oil. Brush the spears with marinade while broiling.

COMBINATION I

Alternate beef chunks, parboiled chunks of leek, whole mushrooms, and a cauliflower blossom, which has been blanched.

COMBINATION II

Alternate beef cubes, small white onions (parboiled), red and green pepper squares.

COMBINATION III

Alternate small oysters wrapped in bacon, water chestnuts, mushroom caps and cubes of ham.

CHINESE-STYLE BEEF WITH GREEN PEPPERS

This recipe has many ingredients, but once you gather them, the dish is cooked in a short time and is very tasty.

MARINADE:

4 tablespoons soy sauce　　　*2 pounds beef tenderloin*
4 tablespoons sherry　　　　*(it cuts best while meat*
2 tablespoons sesame oil　　*is frozen)*
2 tablespoons water

Blend all the marinade ingredients. Remove fat and fibrous tissue from the meat. Make ¼″ slices across the grain. Marinate for 1 hour.

Assemble the following ingredients:

Oil for frying
6 green peppers, cut in
large chunks
4 tablespoons green
onions, chopped
2 tablespoons gingerroot,
minced

2 teaspoons sugar
2 tablespoons garlic, minced
2 tablespoons black beans,
chopped*
2 teaspoons cornstarch
⅓ cup beef stock**

Drain the beef and save the marinade.

Heat a little oil in large skillet or wok and sauté the beef slices quickly. Add the vegetables and seasonings. Stir-fry briefly. Add the marinade. Add the stock, in which you've dissolved the cornstarch. Blend well and cook until thickened. Taste for seasoning and serve.

HAM-FILLED MUSHROOM CAPS

These wonderful snacks are simple to make and quite unusual.

2 pounds fresh large
mushrooms
¼ cup butter
1½ pounds ham, cooked
and ground

½ cup sour cream
2 tablespoons chives, minced
6 pimento-stuffed green olives,
sliced, for garnish

* Buy them at a Chinese grocery store.
** Made from 1 tablespoon of beef base or bouillon cube, in water.

Preheat oven to 350°. Butter a baking pan. Wash and separate the mushroom caps from the stems. Finely chop enough stems to make 1 cup. Lightly sauté the mushroom caps in melted butter.

Mix together the ham, sour cream, chives and mushroom stems. Mound the mixture liberally in the mushroom caps. Place in a pan and bake for 10 minutes.

Garnish each mushroom with an olive slice. Serve in paper candy cups if desired.

HAM KABOBS

1 cup soy sauce
4 tablespoons dry sherry
1 teaspoon fresh ginger,
   diced
2 tablespoons sugar
1 pound lean cooked ham,
   in 1½" cubes

2 thick slices fresh
   pineapple, cut in chunks
12 preserved kumquats
Fresh mint sprigs for garnish

Mix together the soy sauce, sherry, ginger and sugar. Marinate the ham in this for at least 30 minutes.

Thread six 8" skewers with ham, pineapple and kumquats, and brush with the marinade. Broil 3 inches from heat for 5 minutes, turn to brown and brush again with the marinade.

Garnish with mint to serve.

COCKTAIL FRANKS

These look like the standard frank dish, but their piquant taste is a wonderful surprise. Serve in a chafing dish or in a bowl on a hot tray. Guests can spear them with cocktail forks.

1 pound cocktail franks
5 ounces red-currant jelly
  (half of standard small
  jar)

1 tablespoon prepared
  mustard
Juice of 1 lemon

Boil the franks for about 5 minutes. Drain.

In a small saucepan, combine the jelly, mustard and lemon juice. Bring to a boil. Add the cooked franks. Let them heat thoroughly and become glazed.

Place franks with sauce in a serving dish.

SEAFOOD

RED-CAVIAR MOUSSE

You can prepare this as 24 individual bite-size snacks using 2″ muffin pans, or mold in a fish form. Either way, it is delicious!

6-ounce jar red salmon
  caviar
¼ cup parsley, chopped
1 tablespoon onion, grated
Juice of 1 lemon
1 teaspoon grated lemon
  peel
3 green onions, tops only,
  finely sliced
3 tablespoons cucumber,
  peeled, seeded, finely diced

2 cups sour cream
2 tablespoons plain gelatin
  (2 envelopes)
¼ cup cold water
1 cup heavy cream,
  stiffly whipped
1 teaspoon oil, to grease
3 tablespoons pitted black
  olives, sliced, for garnish
Watercress and a whole
  cucumber for garnish

In a bowl, combine the caviar, parsley, onion, lemon juice, lemon peel, green onions and cucumber. Fold in the sour cream.

Mix the gelatin in water. Dissolve over low heat. Cool. Blend into the whipped cream. Fold this into the caviar mixture.

Put the mousse into a medium-size fish form or into muffin-pan cups that have been slightly oiled. Chill until solid.

To serve: Unmold the fish form on a platter. Garnish with thin slices of black olives to simulate fish scales. Surround mold with sprigs of watercress.

Wash an unpeeled cucumber. Scrape the cuke lengthwise with the tines of a fork to give a serrated edge. Slice the cucumber and use the rounds as a garnish around the fish mold. Serve with sliced cocktail bread.

When making individual servings, unmold the muffin pan and put each mold on a thin slice of cocktail rye bread. Garnish with black olives, watercress and cucumber as for the large mold.

BASIC BLINI RECIPE

Blinis are always a treat and they're fun to make! Use a 6" crêpe pan. This is an appetizer crêpe.

¾ cup flour	*¾ cup milk, scalded and tepid*
1 teaspoon salt	*2 tablespoons heavy cream*
1 egg, separated	*2 tablespoons dill weed,*
½ yeast cake	*or minced chives*

In a large bowl, mix the flour, salt and egg yolk. Add yeast that has been dissolved in milk, stirring with a wooden spoon. Cover the bowl and let it stand at room temperature for about 2 hours.

Beat the egg white until stiff and fold into the batter. Just before cooking, add the cream and herbs.

Prepare the crêpe pan with nonstick spray or oil or butter. Wipe off excess fat with a paper towel.

Preheat the pan. Pour in enough batter to cover the bottom of the pan and spill off excess. Brown on one side. Flip the crêpe and brown on the other side. Turn the finished crêpe onto counter and cover with a tea towel. Continue making crêpes until all the batter has been used. Yields about 18 crêpes.

CAVIAR OR SMOKED-SALMON BLINI

Use Basic Blini Recipe.

FILLING:

1 cup sour cream	*or*	*3 ounces cream cheese*
4 ounces black caviar		*6 ounces smoked salmon*

For serving, stack the crêpes and let guests fill their own; or make a platter of crêpes, spread and rolled with caviar, topped with sour cream; or spread crêpes with minced salmon and cream-cheese mixture and roll.

You can, for snacks, roll the blinis, then cut them in 1"-thick slices. Stick a cocktail pick through each slice for easy eating.

The whole rolls can be frozen and sliced at serving time. Serve at room temperature or warm. They thaw quickly and hold up well.

CLAM CRISPS

1 cup flour
1 teaspoon baking powder
¼ teaspoon cayenne
2 eggs
½ cup milk
2 cups fresh or canned
  clams, drained and
  minced

¼ cup scallions, minced
1 tablespoon parsley, minced
Salt and pepper
Peanut oil for French-frying
Red cocktail sauce and
  tartar sauce

Sift together the flour, baking powder and cayenne. Blend the eggs and milk into the flour mixture until smooth. Let stand covered for 30 minutes.

Mix the clams, scallions and parsley into the batter. Salt and pepper to taste.

Preheat the oil to 375°. Drop the batter by tablespoonfuls into the oil. Fry to golden brown, turning once. Remove with slotted spoon to paper towels to drain. Serve with bowls of red Cocktail Sauce (page 65) and Tartar Sauce (page 75).

AVOCADO STUFFED WITH CRABMEAT

3 avocados
Juice of 1 lemon
¾ pound crabmeat
½ cup Thousand Island
   dressing

1 egg yolk, hard-cooked
12 black olives
Greens and cherry tomatoes
   for garnish

Cut the avocados in halves or quarters. Dip the surfaces in lemon juice.

Mix together the crabmeat and dressing. Fill the avocado cavities with mounds of crab mixture.

Garnish with the sieved egg yolk and black olive wedges. Serve on a platter of greens. Add cherry tomatoes for color.

THOUSAND ISLAND DRESSING:

½ cup mayonnaise
2 tablespoons ketchup
2 tablespoons chili sauce
Dash of Tabasco
1 tablespoon
   Worcestershire sauce

2 hard-cooked eggs,
   finely chopped
2 tablespoons sour cream
Salt and pepper to taste

Blend all ingredients. Keep chilled until ready to use.

CRABMEAT DOTLETS

Enjoy this great tidbit as we do!
  Use Choux Paste recipe (page 213) to make 2 dozen dotlet shells.

FILLING:

2 tablespoons butter
2 tablespoons onion,
  finely diced
½ cup fresh mushrooms,
  finely chopped
2 tablespoons flour
½ teaspoon salt

⅛ teaspoon chili powder
Dash of Tabasco sauce
¾ cup milk
6 ounces crabmeat,
  coarsely chopped
2 tablespoons Cheddar
  cheese, grated

In a skillet, melt the butter, add the onion and sauté until golden brown. Add the mushrooms and sauté for 5 minutes. Add the flour and seasonings. Stir until smooth. Add the milk and stir until thickened. Remove from heat, blend in the crabmeat. Cool. Taste for seasoning.

  Fill the dotlet shells. Replace pastry cap or leave open as desired. Up to this point these can be made in advance and refrigerated.

To serve: Preheat oven to 350°. Place the dotlets on a cookie sheet and bake for 10 minutes. During the last few minutes, sprinkle each dotlet with the cheese. Keep in the oven until the cheese melts.

48

CRABMEAT QUICHE

PASTRY:

2 cups flour
½ teaspoon salt
4 tablespoons cold butter

5 tablespoons shortening
1 egg, beaten
6 tablespoons ice water

Preheat oven to 450°. Have ready a deep 10″ pie pan.

In a bowl, combine the flour, salt, butter and shortening. Work these ingredients with your fingertips until crumbly. Add the egg and blend. Using a knife, cut in the ice water until the ingredients form a ball. On a lightly floured board, roll out the dough and fit into your pie pan. Chill while preparing filling.

CRABMEAT FILLING:

1½ cups fresh crabmeat
2 tablespoons parsley,
   minced
2 tablespoons vermouth
½ teaspoon salt
⅛ teaspoon white pepper

¼ teaspoon rosemary
Dash of Tabasco sauce
4 eggs
1½ cups half-and-half
   cream
Paprika

In a bowl, combine the crabmeat, parsley, vermouth, salt, pepper, rosemary and Tabasco sauce. Put this mixture into the unbaked crust.

Beat the eggs lightly and add the cream. Blend and pour over the crabmeat mixture. Sprinkle with paprika. Bake at 450° for 10 minutes, reduce the heat to 350°. Bake for 20 minutes longer, or until knife inserted in the center comes out clean.

Cool. Cut into 12 portions. You may serve the quiche either cool or warm. It freezes well.

CRABMEAT BALLS

These were always a great favorite in my restaurant.

3 tablespoons butter	Salt and pepper
5 tablespoons flour	½ cup mayonnaise
1 cup light cream	1 cup bread crumbs
1 teaspoon celery salt	Oil
1 small onion, grated	Watercress and lemon wedges
Juice of 1 lemon	for garnish
2 egg yolks	
3 cups crabmeat,	
well drained	

In a large skillet, melt the butter, add the flour and stir. Continue stirring while gradually adding cream, celery salt, onion and lemon juice. Cook until thickened, for about 5 minutes. Carefully stir in the egg yolks. Add the crabmeat. Salt and pepper to taste. Remove from the heat and cool. Form into balls the size of a walnut. Cover each ball with mayonnaise and roll in crumbs.

Preheat oil to 375°. Gently fry a few balls at a time. When golden brown, drain on paper towels. Keep warm in 150° oven until all crab balls are ready. Serve on a large platter. Garnish with watercress and lemon wedges.

CRABMEAT OR BACON TARTLETS

Use Tartlet recipe (page 104) for 24 small shells.

FILLING:

2 cups light cream
2 whole eggs plus 2 yolks
½ cup Swiss cheese,
  grated
½ cup sharp Cheddar
  cheese, grated
2 teaspoons
  Worcestershire sauce
Dash of nutmeg

2 tablespoons vermouth
Salt and pepper
4 strips of bacon, crisply
  cooked and crumbled
6 ounces crabmeat, shredded
Sprinkling of paprika and
  lemon dill (or lemon juice
  and dill)

Preheat oven to 400°. Scald the cream. Remove from the heat and cool slightly. Beat the eggs and yolks. Stir into the cream with the cheese and seasonings.

Divide the mixture in two 8″ pie plates. Stir the bacon in one and crabmeat in the other. Set the pans in a tray of water and bake for 15 minutes, or until a knife stuck in the center of the pan comes out clean. When the filling is baked, with a teaspoon fill each tartlet shell generously. Sprinkle with paprika and lemon dill. Serve warm.

WON TON BUTTERFLIES

Make plenty of these because they will disappear quickly! You can find won ton wrappers in a Chinese grocery. They are about 3" square. This recipe uses half a package.

1 pound package frozen　　　*Oil for frying*
　　won ton wrappers

FILLING:

1 pound crabmeat　　　　*1 teaspoon*
4 ounces cream cheese　　　*Worcestershire sauce*
2 teaspoons soy sauce　　*Juice of 1 lemon*

Combine all the filling ingredients and blend thoroughly. Have a bowl of cold water at hand.

In the center of each won ton square, put 1 tablespoon of filling. Moisten the edges with cold water and fold over into a triangle. Again moisten the center of the triangle. Using your index fingers and thumbs, grasp the long ends of the dough and bring your fingers together. Press hard so the dough sticks. Now you have a butterfly with little wings extended.

Fry the won tons in hot oil in a deep skillet until golden brown. Drain on paper towels.

Should you prefer to make these ahead, after frying and draining, place the won tons on a baking sheet and reheat in a 200° oven. Do not cover, or they will lose their crispness.

🌸

CRAB-AND-SHRIMP MOUSSE

This is attractive made in a fish mold. Use as a spread served with assorted crackers.

1 small can tomato soup
1 3-ounce package lemon
* gelatin*
1 pound crabmeat, cooked
1½ pounds tiny shrimp,
* cooked*
½ cup celery, diced
1 large shallot, grated

¾ cup mayonnaise,
* preferably homemade*
2 tablespoons sour cream
¾ cup chili sauce
Salt and pepper to taste
Parsley, lemon wedges,
* butter lettuce and*
* black olives for garnish*

Heat the concentrated (undiluted) tomato soup. Add the gelatin. Stir until dissolved. Set aside.

Mix together all the other ingredients. Blend in the gelatin mixture. Pour into an oiled fish mold. Chill for several hours or overnight.

When ready to serve, unmold on a platter. Garnish with the parsley, lemon wedges, butter lettuce and black olives.

ESCARGOT-STUFFED MUSHROOMS

1 7-ounce can escargots,
  drained
¼ cup white vinegar
¾ cup olive oil
1 garlic clove, minced
1 teaspoon fresh parsley,
  minced
2 tablespoons chives,
  chopped

1 teaspoon salt
24 medium-size mushroom
  caps
1 tablespoon butter
Juice of 1 lemon
Toast rounds

Marinate the snails in a vinaigrette dressing made by mixing the vinegar, oil, garlic, parsley, 1 tablespoon of the chives and salt. Chill for at least 1 hour.

Sauté the mushroom caps in the butter and lemon juice for 5 minutes.

Drain the escargots. Insert one in each mushroom. Sprinkle with the remaining chives. Serve cold on toast rounds.

FISH KABOBS

Use 8″ skewers for this fresh, simple dish.

¾ cup salad oil	Salt and pepper
½ cup fresh lemon juice	2 pounds halibut, cut in
1 bay leaf, crumbled	1½″ cubes
2 teaspoons fresh dill,	2 cucumbers, in 1″ slices
minced, or dill weed	24 pimento-stuffed green
4 drops Tabasco sauce	olives
2 teaspoons instant	4 tablespoons chives, minced
minced onion	

Make a marinade of the oil, lemon juice, bay leaf, dill, Tabasco sauce, onion, salt and pepper. Add the fish cubes. Marinate for 30 minutes at room temperature.

Remove the fish. Boil the marinade for 10 minutes. Add the fish and boil for 10 minutes longer. Drain the fish. Save the marinade.

Thread the fish on 8″ skewers alternately with the cucumber slices and olives. Brush liberally with the marinade and sprinkle with chives. Serve.

Put the rest of the marinade in a bowl for additional dipping, if guests desire.

FISH QUENELLES WITH SHRIMP SAUCE

This dish involves quite a lot of time and several different preparations, which come together to produce a super dish! It will receive raves, and for me that makes the work worthwhile.

MAKE A PANADE:

1 cup milk   1½ cups flour
3 tablespoons butter

In a heavy saucepan, bring the milk and butter to a boil. Add the flour all at once. Remove the pan from the heat. With a wooden spoon, stir the mixture until it leaves the side of the pan. This is your panade. Spread it in a lightly buttered shallow dish. Cover with plastic wrap and chill for at least 1 hour.

MAKE A STOCK:

1 tablespoon salt   ½ celery root, sliced, or ½
1 large onion   bunch celery, coarsely diced
2 large carrots

Fill a large pot with 3 quarts of water. Add all stock ingredients. Bring to a rolling boil over high heat. Reduce the heat and keep the stock at a bare simmer.

MAKE THE FISH QUENELLES:

¾ pound filet of sole   *¼ teaspoon nutmeg*
½ pound salmon filet   *5 eggs, lightly beaten*
1 tablespoon salt   *3 egg whites*
½ teaspoon white pepper   *5 tablespoons butter, softened*

Cut the fish into small pieces and place them in a blender or food processor. Purée the fish with seasonings, beaten eggs and egg whites. Add the panade, cut into small pieces, and the butter. Blend until the mixture is smooth. Put into a bowl. Correct seasoning if necessary.

Dip two soup spoons in the hot stock to heat them. Fill the spoons with the fish mixture to form a quenelle (egg shape). Drop the quenelles into the hot stock, a few at a time, dipping your spoons between each one. Poach the quenelles at a simmer for 10 to 15 minutes, or until they rise to the top and roll over. Transfer them with a slotted spoon to a bowl of cold water. When cooled, put quenelles in a shallow dish and cover.

Proceed to make quenelles from all of the fish mixture. Save the stock.

MAKE A VELOUTÉ SAUCE:

3 tablespoons butter   *½ cup heavy cream*
1 medium onion   *Salt and white pepper*
¼ cup flour
3 cups reserved fish stock,
   strained

In a heavy saucepan, melt the butter, then add the onion and sauté until golden. Gradually stir in flour, and continue to stir and cook for 5 minutes. Remove the pan from the heat and carefully pour in the fish stock, whisking vigorously until the mixture is thick and smooth. Stir in the cream. Add salt and pepper.

Return to the burner and simmer for about 15 minutes.

MAKE A SHRIMP BUTTER:

5 tablespoons butter
½ pound raw shrimp in
   the shell, coarsely
   chopped

3 tablespoons dry white
   wine
Salt and pepper

In a skillet, sauté the shrimp in 2 tablespoons of the butter for 5 minutes, or until cooked. Transfer them to a blender.

Deglaze the skillet with the wine and remaining butter over high heat. Pour over the shrimp in a blender and purée (with the shells). Season to taste.

Strain this mixture through a fine sieve. You should have about ⅓ cup shrimp butter.

MAKE A DUXELLE:

2 tablespoons butter
2 tablespoons oil
½ cup onion, minced
¼ cup shallots, minced

1 pound fresh mushrooms,
   washed and dried, finely
   chopped
Salt and pepper

In a skillet, heat the butter and oil. Sauté the onion and shallots until golden. Add the mushrooms and cook until moisture has evaporated. Season to taste.

Garnish:

½ pound shrimp, cooked,   *Pitted black olives, sliced*
*   shelled and deveined*   *Parsley*

To serve fish quenelles: In a large chafing dish, over moderate heat, pour in the velouté sauce. Add the shrimp butter and the duxelle. Place the fish quenelles in the sauce. Stir occasionally to prevent sticking if dish is standing over heat.

Garnish with shrimp. Sprinkle over sliced olives and put in a few sprigs of parsley.

GEFILLTE FISH BALLS

This recipe will give you 80 to 100 balls depending on how small they are; you can make larger balls and slice or cube them for serving.

Use horseradish to accompany the fish balls. If you like the red horseradish and cannot buy it, add the juice of canned beets.

The fish balls freeze well. Freeze them with some of the stock, then reheat them in the stock and cool for serving.

The flavor of gefillte fish balls varies with the geography. In different parts of the country, by necessity, you'll be using different fish combinations. You

need a fat fish and a lean fish. In the Middle West we used Lake Superior
white fish with pike or pickerel, and that's what they do in New York. On the
West Coast, we use Chinook salmon with sole.

FISH STOCK:

4 onions, cut up

1 bunch celery, coarsely
    sliced

6 carrots, pared and sliced

1 bunch parsley, tied in
    cheesecloth

Head and bones from
    the fish

2 teaspoons sugar

Salt and white pepper
    to taste

Put all the ingredients in a large kettle, cover with cold water, bring to a boil
and let cook gently while preparing fish mixture.

FISH MIXTURE:

6 pounds Chinook fresh
    salmon filets*

3 pounds filet of sole*

3 pounds white onions

10 large eggs

¼ cup matzo meal

¼ cup cold water

2 teaspoons sugar

Salt and white pepper to taste

* Or any combination of fat and lean fish.

Grind the fish and the onions and place in a large bowl. Add the eggs, one at a time, while beating the mixture. Add the matzo meal, water and seasonings.

As you beat, the mixture gets thicker. It should be of a consistency to handle. If it is too loose, carefully add small amounts of matzo meal.

Dip a small ice cream scoop in cold water and then fill it with the fish mixture, which you drop into the boiling fish stock. Keep on making the balls and dropping them into the stock until all the fish is used. (You can also shape the balls with your hands. Dip your hands in cold water between each ball.)

Cover the kettle and cook on medium heat for about 1½ hours. Turn off the heat and let the balls remain in the stock for 1 more hour. Carefully remove the balls, placing them in a large container. Strain the stock and pour over the fish balls. When cool, refrigerate.

Serve warm or cold, with horseradish. Egg Twist, or Challah (see page 224) is a good bread to serve with the fish.

HERRING-STUFFED BEETS

*2 15-ounce cans of pickled
    whole beets
1 6-ounce jar herring filets
    in wine sauce, diced*

*1 small onion, diced
½ pint sour cream*

With a melon baller, scoop a ball from the top of each beet. Mix the herring and onion and fill the beet cavity. Garnish with a teaspoonful of sour cream. Serve with sliced dark bread.

HERRING IN SOUR CREAM

This is very easy to make and is a tangy, memorable dish.

1 8-ounce jar pickled   *4 tablespoons white wine*
    herring filets   *1 teaspoon sugar*
½ Bermuda onion, thinly   *Juice of 1 lemon*
    sliced   *Salt and pepper*
6 tablespoons sour cream

Drain the herring and put into a bowl with the onion. Blend all the other ingredients and pour over herring. Serve with pumpernickel bread.

CHOPPED HERRING SALAD

This is a great-tasting spread on thinly sliced rye or pumpernickel bread.

1 8-ounce jar of herring   *1 slice of rye bread*
    filets in wine sauce   *¼ cup vinegar*
1 small onion   *6 eggs, hard-cooked*
1 unpeeled apple, cored   *Salt and pepper*

Drain the herring filets. In a food processor or blender, chop the herring, onion, apple, rye bread soaked in the vinegar, and 4 of the eggs. Season to taste.

Serve in a large bowl garnished, if you like, with onion and green-pepper rings, slices of the remaining eggs and, around it, beet buds and parsley.

HERRING RING FILLED WITH SHRIMP

Eating this dish is a sophisticated gourmet experience.

*1 small bottle
  pimento-stuffed
  green olives, sliced
1 12-ounce jar pickled
  herring filets, drained
1 7-ounce can tuna fish,
  drained
1 tablespoon onion, grated
1 tablespoon lemon juice
Salt and pepper to taste*

*4 tablespoons sweet butter,
  at room temperature
2 pounds fresh shrimp,
  cooked, deveined and
  marinated in Cocktail
  Sauce (page 80)
1 can artichoke bottoms
1 2-ounce jar black caviar
Parsley, lemon wedges and
  cherry tomatoes for garnish*

Place a border of olive slices in the bottom of an oiled 1-quart ring mold.

Combine the herring, tuna, onion and lemon juice in a blender or food processor to get a smooth mixture. Salt and pepper to taste. Stir in the softened butter. Spoo_ some of the mixture over the olive slices in the mold to hold them in place, then pour in the rest of it. Refrigerate until set.

63

To serve: Unmold on a large parsley-lined platter. Fill the center with the marinated shrimp. Surround the mold with artichoke bottoms topped with black caviar, lemon wedges and cherry tomatoes.

Serve with dark breads and assorted crackers.

OYSTERS ROCKEFELLER

We used these as a first course for my son's wedding dinner and they were enthusiastically received. They are great also as a buffet pickup.

10 large oysters in the
shell
1 bunch parsley
½ cup spinach, cooked
and well drained
1 green pepper
1 teaspoon lemon juice
1 tablespoon
Worcestershire sauce

½ teaspoon salt
2 cloves garlic, minced
Cocktail sauce
2 tablespoons butter
¼ cup cracker crumbs
5 slices of bacon
Rock salt

Open the oysters, leaving them on the half shell. Chop together the parsley, spinach and green pepper. Add the lemon juice, Worcestershire sauce, salt and minced garlic. Mix in enough cocktail sauce (see below) to form a paste.

Cover each oyster with about 1 tablespoon of the mixture. Melt the butter and pour it over the cracker crumbs. Sprinkle each oyster with crumbs. Cut each bacon strip into 8 pieces. Place 4 small pieces of bacon over each oyster.

Cover the bottom of a baking pan with rock salt. Place the prepared oyster shells on the salt. Broil until the bacon is well browned.

COCKTAIL SAUCE:

1 cup chili sauce
½ cup ketchup
2 tablespoons horseradish
1 tablespoon
  Worcestershire sauce

Juice of 1 lemon
Dash of Tabasco sauce

Blend all the ingredients. Chill and use as needed. Keeps well in the refrigerator.

OYSTERS BAKED ON THE HALF SHELL

2 cloves garlic, minced
2 tablespoons butter, at
  room temperature
2 tablespoons dry white
  wine
2 teaspoons Maggi sauce

2 teaspoons
  Worcestershire sauce
Dash of salt
4 tablespoons Parmesan
  cheese, grated
2 dozen fresh oysters

Preheat oven to 350°. Mix the garlic, butter, wine, Maggi and Worcestershire sauces and salt into a paste.

Open each oyster, leave it in its half shell and spread it with the paste. Sprinkle heavily with grated cheese. Bake for about 10 minutes, or until the cheese is brown.

SCALLOPED OYSTERS

DELISH!

6 tablespoons butter
2 cups salted cracker
    crumbs
4 shallots, diced
2 cups fresh mushrooms,
    sliced

1 pint oysters, drained
    (save juice)
1 cup cream
Dash of white pepper
½ cup parsley, chopped

Preheat oven to 375°. Melt 4 tablespoons of the butter and blend with the cracker crumbs.

In a skillet, sauté the shallots in the remaining butter until golden. Add the mushrooms and cook for 5 minutes.

Spread half the buttered crumbs on bottom of a greased ½-quart baking dish. Put the oysters over the crumbs. Cover the oysters with the mushroom mixture. Pour over the oyster juice, plus the cream. Add a dash of pepper. Top with the rest of the crumbs and sprinkle with parsley.

Bake for 45 minutes.

PRAWNS IN ARTICHOKE

This attractive and excellent appetizer can be made ahead of time and refrigerated. The artichoke is used for presentation only.

TO PREPARE ARTICHOKE:

2 large fresh artichokes   Juice of 2 lemons
2 tablespoons salt

Slice off the stem to make the artichoke level. With scissors, cut off the tips of each artichoke.

In a large saucepan, put 1 quart of water, add salt, lemon juice and artichokes. Bring to a boil and cook for 10 minutes. Remove the artichokes from the liquid, turn upside down to drain well. Put aside in the refrigerator.

TO PREPARE SHRIMP:

1½ pounds medium   1 bay leaf
   shrimp, raw in shell   6 whole allspice
1 large onion, cut up   Salt and pepper
1 clove garlic, chopped   1 lemon, sliced

Put all the ingredients except the shrimp in 1 quart of water and boil for 10 minutes. Add the shrimp and boil only until the shrimp turn pink. Turn off the heat and let the shrimp remain in the broth until cool. Peel and devein the shrimp.

TO PREPARE SAUCE:

1 tablespoon gelatin
  (one envelope)
2 tablespoons cold water
½ cup ketchup
½ cup chili sauce

1 teaspoon
  Worcestershire sauce
1 teaspoon horseradish
Dash of Tabasco sauce
Juice of 1 lemon

Mix the gelatin with the water in top of a double boiler and dissolve over boiling water. Cool.

Mix all the other ingredients, add the gelatin and chill for 1 hour.

To assemble: Cover a platter with sprigs of watercress or parsley. Place the artichokes upright on the greens. Dip each shrimp into the chilled cocktail sauce and then tuck a shrimp behind each petal of the artichoke until the artichoke is completely filled. Carefully add a little additional sauce if you think it's needed. Chill again before using. Serve with cocktail picks on buffet table.

PRAWNS À LA FLAMINGO

Serve with picks or small forks and your guests will happily spear these delicacies.

24 large prawns or shrimp, raw
2 tablespoons butter
1 large carrot, minced

2 leeks, minced
½ cup dry sauterne
1 cup half-and-half cream

Sauté the prawns in 1 tablespoon of the butter until half cooked. Add the carrots and leeks with the remaining butter. Sauté quickly until the vegetables are half cooked. Add the wine and cream. Simmer until the vegetables and prawns are tender.

DRY ROUX:

1 tablespoon butter	*½ teaspoon salt*
1 tablespoon flour	*¼ teaspoon white pepper*

Mix all the ingredients and stir into the hot prawn mixture. Cook for another couple of minutes until sauce thickens slightly.

SALMON-AND-STURGEON MOUSSE

I think you will find this is a very exciting dish.

1 pound fresh salmon filets	*1 onion, diced*
1 pound fresh sturgeon filets	*2 egg whites*
Salt and white pepper	*1 tablespoon butter, at room temperature*
Juice of 2 lemons	*Parsley and paprika for garnish*

Preheat oven to 350°. Slice the fish into ¼″ pieces. Salt and pepper, and sprinkle about two thirds of the fish with half the lemon juice. Set aside.

Put the rest of the fish in a blender or food processor with the onion, remaining lemon juice, salt and pepper, and egg whites. Blend to a purée.

Line a well-greased 2-quart baking dish with half of the cut-up fish filets. Cover with the fish purée. Place the remaining fish filets over the purée. Cover the fish dish with a piece of buttered wax paper, set the dish in a pan of water and bake for about 1 hour.

Before serving, spoon a little of the fish sauce over the baked mousse. Garnish with parsley and paprika.

FISH SAUCE FOR MOUSSE:

2 tablespoons butter	4 ounces clam juice
1 medium onion, diced	½ pound tiny cooked shrimp
1 tablespoon flour	2 egg yolks
Juice of 1 lemon	½ cup heavy cream
½ cup white wine	Salt and white pepper

In a deep skillet, melt the butter, add the onion and sauté until golden. Blend in the flour, lemon juice, wine and clam juice. Keep stirring over moderate heat. Add the shrimp. Lastly and carefully, stir in the egg yolks mixed with the cream.

Simmer until the mixture is just heated through, but do not let it come to a boil.

Pour some of the sauce over the mousse; serve the rest of it in a bowl on the side.

LOX ROULADES (SMOKED SALMON)

½ pound lox, thinly
  sliced
¼ pound cream cheese,
  at room temperature

1 Bermuda onion, thinly
  sliced
Parsley and black olives
  for garnish

Spread pieces of lox, about 2″ x 3″, with a thin layer of cream cheese. Roll lengthwise. Arrange on a platter and garnish with raw onion rings, parsley and olives.

Serve with thin slices of pumpernickel or split bagels.

SMOKED-SALMON SPREAD

¾ pound Nova Scotia
  smoked salmon or lox
¾ cup sweet butter,
  melted and cooled
1½ teaspoons anchovy
  paste

1½ teaspoons lemon juice
1 tablespoon dill weed
Toast rounds
Capers for garnish

Set aside 1 small slice of salmon for garnish.

In a blender or food processor, purée the salmon with the butter, anchovy paste and lemon juice. Add the dill weed. Chill the mixture until it is firm, but still of spreading consistency.

When ready to serve, spread on toast rounds. Top each with a small piece of salmon and a caper.

SARDINE-AND-CHEESE PUFFS

These are delicious and so simple to make.

1 loaf white sandwich bread, unsliced
8 ounces boneless and skinless sardines, drained (about 2 small cans)

1 teaspoon grated onion
Juice of 1 lemon
8 ounces cream cheese
1 egg yolk
½ teaspoon baking powder
Salt and paprika

Decrust the bread and cut in thin slices. Toast the slices in the oven on one side.

Blend the sardines, onion, lemon juice, cheese, egg yolk and baking powder. Add salt and paprika to taste. Spread the untoasted side of the bread with this mixture.

Just before serving, put under the broiler until puffed and brown. Watch carefully so they don't burn.

Cut each slice in fingerlengths and serve.

SARDINE PINEAPPLES

These are pretty, easy to pick up and wonderful to eat. You can glaze them if you like.

8 ounces boneless and
   skinless sardines (about
   2 small cans)
4 ounces cream cheese
Juice of 1 lemon

½ small onion, grated
12 small pimento-stuffed
   green olives
Small leaves from top of
   fresh pineapple

Drain the sardines thoroughly and put them in a small bowl. Add the cream cheese, lemon juice and onion. Blend well. Take 2 teaspoons of this mixture in the palm of your hand, and using both hands, roll into a ball, then shape into a cone resembling a pineapple. Slice the olives as thinly as possible. Cover each sardine cone completely with olive slices. Top each one with small sprigs of real pineapple leaves. Place each little pineapple in a paper candy cup.

GLAZE:

1 tablespoon unflavored
   gelatin

4 tablespoons cold water
1 tablespoon lemon juice

Dissolve unflavored gelatin in cold water. After 5 minutes, place in a double boiler over hot water to melt. Add the lemon juice. When partially thickened, brush this glaze over the little "pineapples." You may have to repeat this glazing again to make them shiny. Chill.

🌹

LIMED SCALLOPS

If you can find them, use six large scallop shells for individual servings.

3 dozen sea scallops,
medium size
6 tablespoons butter,
melted
Salt and pepper
6 limes, each cut into 6
thin slices

6 thin slices Canadian
bacon, cut in half
6 tablespoons Parmesan
cheese, grated

Preheat oven to 400°. Wash the scallops and dry on paper towels. Put 6 scallops in each shell. Dribble a tablespoon of butter over each serving. Season with salt and pepper.

Place a slice of lime on each scallop. Cover with 2 half slices of the bacon. Sprinkle 1 tablespoon of the cheese over each filled shell.

Bake for about 10 minutes, or until the fish is cooked, bacon browned and cheese melted. Baste the scallops while baking.

Serve with tartar sauce.

TARTAR SAUCE:

1 cup mayonnaise
1 tablespoon parsley,
   finely chopped
1 tablespoon chives,
   chopped
1 tablespoon tarragon,
   fresh or dried

1 tablespoon capers,
   drained
1 small dill pickle,
   finely chopped
3 lemons, for serving,
   halved and hollowed

Blend all the ingredients.

Scoop out the lemon shells. Fill with the sauce and use as a garnish for this and many other fish dishes.

SCALLOPS IN CHAMPAGNE

This dish makes a wonderful snack.

4 tablespoons butter
½ cup shallots, diced
1 bay leaf
Salt and pepper
1½ cups dry champagne
2 pounds scallops
1 pound fresh mushroom
   caps

Juice of 1 lemon
4 tablespoons flour
1 pint French-style sour
   cream (crème fraîche)
4 tablespoons chives, chopped
1 tablespoon paprika

In a deep skillet, melt the butter. Add the shallots, bay leaf, and salt and pepper to taste. Sauté until the shallots are golden. Add champagne and the scallops. Simmer for 10 minutes. Drain the scallops, but save the strained liquid.

In another skillet, steam the mushroom caps and lemon juice, covered, for 5 minutes. Add the scallops. Sprinkle in the flour and stir. Add the sour cream and reserved liquid. Stir until well blended and cook gently until liquid is reduced.

Pour into a chafing dish. Sprinkle with the chives and paprika. Serve with cocktail picks on the side and thin sliced breads.

CRÈME FRAÎCHE:

1½ pints heavy cream   *½ cup sour cream*

Let the fresh cream stand at room temperature for 24 hours. Blend in the sour cream.

SCALLOPS AND VEGETABLE LOLLIPOPS

Use 6″ skewers.

MARINADE:

3 tablespoons sherry   *2 teaspoons sesame oil*
3 slices gingerroot,   *Juice of 1 lemon*
*   smashed*   *1 pound scallops*

Combine all the ingredients and pour over the scallops. Marinate for 1 hour.

4 whole large carrots, *peeled*	*5 whole turnips, peeled* *3 thick zucchini, unpeeled*

Partially cook the carrots, turnips and zucchini in boiling salted water, covered, for about 5 minutes. Remove the vegetables and save the liquid. Using a melon baller, make balls from the vegetables.

To the vegetable liquid, add:

2 teaspoons salt *1 teaspoon sugar*	*1 tablespoon chicken soup base* *1 bay leaf*

Bring this mixture to a boil. Add the scallops. Cook for 5 minutes, add the vegetable balls and cook for 5 minutes more. Drain the scallops and vegetables. Save the stock and bring it to a boil. Add 2 teaspoons of cornstarch dissolved in 1 tablespoon of water. Stir in the cornstarch until the liquid becomes thickened and glazy.

Using 6″ skewers, thread them with, alternately, scallops and vegetable balls. Arrange the skewers on serving plate, on top of toast points. Brush "lollipops" with the hot glaze and serve.

Garnish with parsley, lemon wedges and cherry tomatoes.

SEAFOOD PANCAKE PIE

When making pancakes that I want to fill or spread, I like to keep them soft and pliable. As I make them I stack them on a pie plate set in a skillet of hot water. Keep covered.

BATTER:

4 eggs, separated

1 cup cream

1 cup pastry flour (or all-purpose flour)

½ teaspoon salt

1 tablespoon sugar

¼ teaspoon baking powder

1 tablespoon melted butter

Butter to grease skillet

Beat the egg yolks, add the cream. Sift the dry ingredients and blend into the yolk mixture. Add the melted butter. Beat the egg whites until stiff and blend into the batter.

Heat a 10″ skillet; it should be hot. Wipe with melted butter, using a pastry brush or a paper towel. Pour a little batter into the skillet, tilt the pan back and forth so the batter covers the bottom thinly. When brown, turn and brown the other side.

This recipe makes about 6 pancakes.

FILLING:

8 ounces cream cheese
1 tube anchovy paste
3 ounces smoked salmon
   (lox)

6 ounces salmon caviar
1 teaspoon onion, grated
Juice of 1 lemon

Blend half the cream cheese with the anchovy paste. Mash the rest of the cream cheese with the salmon to make a spread. Mix the caviar with the onion and lemon juice.

To assemble: Place a pancake on a serving plate. Spread with a thin layer of anchovy mixture. Top with another pancake. Spread it with a thin layer of caviar. Top with a pancake. Spread it with a thin layer of salmon spread. Continue stacking the layers until all pancakes are used.

Using a sharp knife, slice pie fashion, but keep intact.

A bowl of Newburg sauce for dipping is nice, but optional.

SHRIMP COCKTAIL

This simple, familiar dish is mouth-watering and an all-time American favorite.

2 pounds fresh shrimp or
   prawns, in shells
4 tablespoons salt
1 bay leaf
6 peppercorns

1 large onion, sliced
1 clove garlic, chopped
3 large sticks of celery, cut up
Bunch of parsley
Juice of 2 lemons

Bring 3 quarts of water to a boil and add all the ingredients except the shrimp. Cook for about 15 minutes. Add the shrimp and boil for about 5 minutes. Remove from the heat, but let the shrimp remain in the water for 10 minutes. Shell and devein the shrimp.

Pour a little cocktail sauce over them and chill thoroughly.

COCKTAIL SAUCE:

1 cup ketchup
1 cup chili sauce
Juice of 1 lemon
1 tablespoon
   Worcestershire sauce

2 teaspoons horseradish
Dash of Tabasco sauce

Blend all the ingredients. Fill a nice bowl with the cocktail sauce and place it in the middle of a large platter on which you have arranged the shrimp on crushed ice. Serve with cocktail picks.

HORSERADISH RING FILLED WITH SHRIMP SALAD

3 tablespoons plain
   gelatin
½ cup vodka
Liquid from 3 #2½ cans
   pickled beet buds
2 tablespoons lemon juice

1 teaspoon celery salt
1 tablespoon horseradish
½ teaspoon dry mustard
2 teaspoons sugar
Salt and pepper to taste
Greens for garnish

Dissolve the gelatin in the vodka. In a saucepan, combine the beet liquid and all other ingredients, including the gelatin, but not the greens, of course. Stir until well blended. Bring to a boil. Pour into an oiled 2-quart ring mold and chill.

When ready to set your buffet, unmold the ring on a platter of greens. Your mold will give you a firm, shallow red ring to fill with shrimp salad.

SHRIMP SALAD:

2 pounds shrimp,
    cooked, shelled and
    deveined
2 cups celery, finely
    sliced
2 cups cucumber,
    seeded, diced
½ cup scallions,
    finely diced

2 teaspoons
    Worcestershire sauce
Juice of 2 lemons
½ cup chili sauce
¼ cup ketchup
Salt and pepper to taste
Lemon wedges and parsley
    for garnish

Combine the shrimp with the celery, cucumber and scallions. Blend the remaining ingredients and combine with the shrimp mixture. Fill the horseradish ring. Garnish with lemon wedges and parsley.

GLAZED SHRIMP

Shrimp, boiled, shelled and
  deveined

ASPIC:

2 tablespoons plain
  gelatin
¼ cup cold water
½ cup vinegar
1 teaspoon
  Worcestershire sauce

2 tablespoons sugar
1 teaspoon salt
1 tablespoon horseradish

Soak the gelatin in the cold water. In a saucepan, combine the rest of the ingredients and bring to a boil. Add the gelatin and stir until it is dissolved. Remove from the heat and let cool.

Using 2" muffin tins, pour 1 teaspoon of aspic into each tin. Refrigerate for about 20 minutes. Add a shrimp, or if using tiny shrimp, three or four. Cover the shrimp with additional aspic. Refrigerate until firm. When ready to serve, remove from the pan.

Use in the "French Bouquet" (see page 107), or serve these glazed shrimp on toast rounds or crackers.

FRENCH-FRIED SHRIMP

1 pound raw shrimp

Shell and devein the shrimp but leave the tail shell on.

BATTER:

1 egg　　　　　　　　　　　*1 teaspoon baking powder*
1 cup milk　　　　　　　　　*1 teaspoon salt*
1 cup flour

Preheat deep fat for frying to 375°. Beat the egg until light. Add the milk alternately with the flour, to which the baking powder and salt have been added. Blend well.

　Holding the shrimp by the tail, dip in the batter. Fry until golden brown. Drain on unglazed paper.

　Serve with a red Cocktail Sauce (page 80).

SESAME SHRIMP EN BROCHETTE

32 prawns or shrimp,
　medium size, shelled
　and deveined

83

MARINADE:

1 cup white wine
½ cup soy sauce
Salt and pepper

Small piece fresh ginger,
minced

Blend ingredients and marinate the shrimp for 2 hours or more.

2 tablespoons butter
16 mushroom caps
Juice of 1 lemon

1 cup sesame seeds
Cherry tomatoes and
parsley for garnish

In a skillet, melt the butter, add the mushroom caps and sprinkle the lemon juice over them. Cover and steam for 5 minutes. Drain.

Using eight 6″ skewers, thread 4 shrimp and 2 mushroom caps on each skewer. Save the marinade.

Roll the kabobs in sesame seeds until well covered. Place on a rack and broil for 5 minutes on each side. Keep warm in 150° oven until ready to serve.

It is nice to use the leftover marinade as a dipping sauce for the kabobs.

To prepare the dipping sauce from the marinade:

Dissolve 1 tablespoon of cornstarch in ¼ cup white wine. Bring the marinade to a boil and add the cornstarch mixture. Stir constantly until glazy. Remove from the heat and pour into a small serving bowl.

Stack the kabobs on a flat platter or stick them into a small head of green cabbage or a grapefruit. (Take a slice from the bottom to make level on the serving plate.) Garnish with cherry tomatoes and parsley. Place the sauce on the side for dipping. When serving these shrimp with other items, you can use shorter skewers with 2 shrimp instead of 4.

SHRIMP WITH BACON

*½ pound fresh medium
    shrimp, cooked and
    deveined*

*½ cup chili sauce
¼ pound bacon, sliced,
    lean*

Marinate the shrimp in the chili sauce.

Wrap each shrimp in half a slice of bacon. Secure with a toothpick. Broil on all sides until the bacon is crisp.

You may want to change to new toothpicks for serving.

BELGIAN ENDIVE SHRIMP BOATS

We get these shrimp fresh in the markets in Portland, but you can substitute canned or frozen shrimp. Just drain them well.

*1 cup mayonnaise
Juice of 1 lemon
2 teaspoons dill weed
1 teaspoon chives, minced*

*Salt and pepper
1 pound cooked tiny shrimp
½ pound Belgian endive*

Blend the mayonnaise, lemon juice, dill weed and chives. Salt and pepper to taste. Add the shrimp.

In the center of a 12″ or 14″ plate, make a mound of the shrimp mixture. Surround the shrimp with washed and dried leaves of the endive like the spokes of a wheel. Each guest fills a spoke with shrimp.

BARBECUED SHRIMP, JAPANESE STYLE

This is a tasty low-calorie Oriental nosh.

> *1 pound uncooked*
> *medium shrimp*
> *(about 24)*

SAUCE:

¼ cup soy sauce
2 tablespoons tomato
juice
1 tablespoon water
1 tablespoon cider
vinegar

½ teaspoon ginger,
ground
Dash of cayenne pepper
2 teaspoons sugar, or
equivalent sugar substitute
1 clove garlic, crushed

Peel and devein the shrimp, leaving tails on. Place in a broiler pan.

In a small saucepan, combine the sauce ingredients. Heat to boiling, reduce the heat and simmer for 3 minutes, uncovered.

Brush the shrimp liberally with the sauce. Broil 4 inches from the heat for about 3 minutes on each side, or until tender. Baste frequently with the sauce and serve hot.

The shrimp may also be put on skewers and grilled over charcoal fire. Baste as when broiling.

🌹

TOASTED SHRIMP ROLLS

These are tasty; one is never enough.

> 1 pound raw medium
>   shrimp, shelled and
>   deveined
> 8 tablespoons butter, at
>   room temperature
>
> 2 tablespoons lemon dill
>   seasoning (or lemon
>   juice and dill)
> 1 loaf white bread, thinly
>   sliced and decrusted

Butterfly the shrimp by slitting them along the outside down to, but not through, the membrane along the underside. Put the split shrimp between sheets of waxed paper. Pound them gently with a wooden mallet.

Spread each shrimp with 1 teaspoon of butter. Sprinkle generously with lemon dill. Roll the shrimp up from the broad end toward the tail and fasten with a toothpick. Chill for two hours.

Roll each slice of decrusted bread until very thin. Place a shrimp roll on each slice and roll the bread up tightly.

Melt the remaining butter. Brush each roll with the melted butter. Broil on all sides until golden brown.

PORCUPINE SHRIMP BALLS

You'll find these interesting and good.

24 medium shrimp,
   cooked, shelled and
   deveined
2 teaspoons dry sherry
1 egg white
¼ teaspoon salt

6 tablespoons flour, or more
1 small can whole water
   chestnuts, drained
3 ounces Chinese noodles,
   brown and crisp*

Preheat peanut oil, 3″ deep, to 375°. Purée the shrimp with sherry in a blender or food processor.

Place the egg white, salt, flour and shrimp purée in a mixing bowl and stir until very smooth. Gradually add more flour if necessary for easier handling. Shape into balls. Make an indentation in each ball and insert ½ of a water chestnut. Roll back into shape, covering the chestnut.

Roll the balls in noodles, letting pieces stick out for a thorny effect. Deep-fry until golden brown, for about 3 minutes. Drain balls on paper towel. Serve at room temperature.

* These come in a can, though the Chinese grocery may package them in a bag.

SHRIMP WITH AVOCADO SAUCE

2 large cucumbers,
   peeled and sliced in
   ¼" rounds
Vinegar dressing
1 pound medium shrimp,
   cooked, shelled and
   deveined
1 small avocado, ripe,
   peeled

3 ounces cream cheese
1 teaspoon lime juice
1 teaspoon dill weed
Salt and white pepper
   to taste
1 egg yolk, hard-cooked
   and sieved

Marinate cucumbers in vinegar dressing. Arrange each shrimp on a slice of prepared cucumber. Thoroughly blend the avocado, cheese, lime juice and dill weed. Season to taste.

   Spoon 1 teaspoon of sauce over each shrimp. Garnish with egg yolk.

VINEGAR DRESSING:

½ cup vinegar
½ small onion, grated
1 teaspoon salt

⅛ teaspoon black pepper
1 tablespoon sugar

Stir all ingredients until sugar dissolves.

SHRIMP DE JONGHE

4 tablespoons butter
1 medium onion, diced
2 cloves garlic, minced
16 fresh medium
  shrimp, shelled,
  deveined
2 tablespoons flour

1 tablespoon parsley,
  chopped
4 ounces Chablis wine
3 tablespoons fresh
  tomatoes, peeled and sliced
Salt and pepper

Preheat oven to 350°. Melt the butter in a skillet. When the foam subsides, add the onion and sauté it until golden brown, then add the garlic. Cook gently for 1 minute, then add the shrimp. Sauté until the shrimp are partially cooked. Blend in the flour. Add the parsley and wine. Let simmer for 3 or 4 minutes. Add the tomatoes and season to taste.

Pour into a small casserole. Bake for 10 minutes and serve.

TUNA-FISH BALLS

1 7-ounce can solid white
   tuna fish, drained
Juice of 1 lemon
¼ cup almonds, blanched
   and toasted
2 tablespoons fresh
   parsley

¼ teaspoon salt
2 tablespoons dry white wine
4 tablespoons fresh chives,
   minced

Combine the tuna with the lemon juice, almonds, parsley and salt in a blender. Add the wine. Blend until smooth. With this mixture, make balls the size of a walnut. Roll the balls in chives.

   Serve in candy cups, with warm toast rounds or crisp crackers on the side.

BAKED TUNA-FISH BALLS WITH DILL SAUCE

2 7-ounce cans of
   solid-pack tuna,
   drained
1 cup bread crumbs
2 eggs
½ cup celery, finely
   chopped
1 medium onion, grated

2 tablespoons parsley,
   chopped
1 tablespoon lemon juice
½ teaspoon salt
½ cup cornflakes, crumbled
1 small jar sweet gherkins
1 small jar stuffed green olives
Parsley

Preheat oven to 350°. Blend together the tuna fish, bread crumbs, eggs, vegetables, lemon juice and salt.

Shape into about 24 balls. Roll them in the cornflake crumbs. Place in a greased shallow baking dish and bake for about 25 minutes, or until lightly browned.

Arrange on a platter and garnish with gherkins, olives and parsley. Serve with a bowl of dill sauce for dipping (use sturdy cocktail picks). Thinly sliced rye bread is also nice with these.

DILL SAUCE:

3 tablespoons butter
1 small bunch green
* onions, chopped*
3 tablespoons flour
1½ cups half-and-half
* cream*

1 tablespoon fresh lemon
* juice*
1 tablespoon dill weed,
* fresh or dried*
Salt and pepper to taste

In a skillet, melt the butter and add the green onions. When golden, blend in the flour and gradually add the half-and-half, stirring constantly. Add the juice, dill and seasoning. Stir until thickened and smooth.

HORS D'OEUVRES
&
DRINKS

STUFFED EGGS

Stuffed eggs can always fill a quick, unexpected "what to serve" situation.

I have found that the easiest method for hard-cooking eggs is to cover the eggs with cold water in a saucepan. Leaving the saucepan uncovered, bring the water to a rolling boil, turn off the heat and let the pan with the eggs remain on the stove for at least 10 minutes. Cool the eggs under running cold water. They should be easy to shell.

An assortment of stuffed eggs makes an interesting and attractive platter.

SALMON-STUFFED EGGS

6 eggs, hard-cooked
⅓ cup fresh salmon,
   cooked and flaked, or
   canned salmon, drained
2 tablespoons mayonnaise
Juice of 1 lemon

1 teaspoon horseradish,
   drained
Salt and pepper to taste
Dill weed
2 black olives, cut
   lengthwise in thin wedges

Split the egg in half lengthwise. Remove yolks carefully and save whites to fill.

In a blender or ꞈ ꞈd processor, purée the yolks, salmon, mayonnaise, lemon juice and horseradish. Add salt and pepper. Chill the mixture for 30 minutes.

95

Mound the filling in the egg whites. Sprinkle with dill weed. Arrange wedges of black olives on each stuffed egg to form a daisy.

PINEAPPLE HAM STUFFED EGGS

6 eggs, hard-cooked
½ cup cooked ham,
    finely minced*
⅓ cup sweet gherkins,
    finely minced*
⅓ cup pineapple, crushed
    and drained*

¼ cup mayonnaise
1 teaspoon prepared mustard,
    Dijon style
Salt and pepper
¼ cup parsley, minced

Split the eggs in half lengthwise. Carefully remove the yolks. Save the whites to fill. Force yolks through a sieve. Blend in the ham, gherkins, pineapple, mayonnaise and mustard. Salt and pepper to taste.

Spoon the mixture into the egg-white halves. Mound them and sprinkle with parsley.

* If you have a food processor, all of these ingredients could be put in to mince and blend.

DEVILED-EGG SHRIMP BASKETS

6 eggs, hard-cooked
1 teaspoon anchovy
 paste
⅓ cup tiny shrimp
1 teaspoon
 Worcestershire sauce

1 tablespoon mayonnaise
6 green-pepper rings
6 pimento-stuffed
 green olives

Cut a thin slice from each end of the eggs so they will sit level.

Using a small paring knife, seesaw-cut each egg in half down the middle. Pull halves apart. Carefully remove the yolks. Save the whites to fill.

Sieve the yolks. Blend in the anchovy paste, shrimp, Worcestershire sauce and mayonnaise. Spoon the mixture into the serrated egg halves, mounding it.

Cut the green-pepper rings in half. Insert the ends of each half into the sides of each filled egg, making a handle for the basket. Slice olives and use as garnish on the egg filling.

EGG BASKET WITH CAVIAR

8 eggs, hard-cooked
3 ounces cream cheese,
  at room temperature
2 tablespoons sour cream
2 tablespoons chives,
  minced

3 tablespoons lemon juice
Salt and pepper
2 tablespoons red caviar
½ of an avocado, not too ripe

Cut the eggs in half lengthwise, remove the yolks. Save the whites to fill.

Sieve the yolks. Blend in the cream cheese, chives, 1 teaspoon lemon juice, salt and pepper to taste. Fold in the caviar. Chill the filling for about 1 hour.

Fill the egg-white cavities by pressing filling through a large star tube in a pastry bag. For a less fancy egg, you can fill the whites with a small spoon.

Slice the half avocado crosswise. Pour the remaining lemon juice over it. Use a slice of avocado to make a handle for each egg "basket."

MACADAMIA CHEESE BALLS

¼ pound blue cheese,
  at room temperature
½ pound medium-sharp
  Cheddar cheese, grated
½ pound cream cheese,
  at room temperature

¼ cup milk
1 teaspoon chutney
1 cup macadamia nuts,
  salted and chopped

Blend the cheeses, milk and chutney. Chill until firm. Spoon into balls about 1" in diameter. Roll each ball in the nuts.

Serve with unsalted, water-type crackers.

FRIED CHEESE BALLS

These were especially popular during the cocktail hour in our lounge at the restaurant. Watch the expression on your guests' faces with the first bite.

The nice part is that you can make the balls ready to fry ahead of time.

1½ cups sharp Cheddar	*Dash of cayenne pepper*
cheese, grated	*3 egg whites, stiffly beaten*
1 tablespoon flour	*Cracker meal*
¼ teaspoon salt	

Preheat shortening or oil to 375°. Blend the cheese, flour and seasonings. Fold in the egg whites. Shape into small balls the size of a walnut. Roll each ball in cracker meal and deep-fry in the preheated oil until golden brown.

Drain on unglazed brown paper. Arrange on a platter with cocktail picks on the side.

ASSORTED CHEESE PLATTER

Cheeses are a popular snack food. This is a suggestion for an assortment of cheeses of varied flavors and textures. I like to use a cheese rose as a center-piece for a partyfied cheese plate; you can make it ahead of time and refrigerate it.

Arrange chunks of cheese. An outside garnish of Cheddar carrots and Cheddar crabapples adds further interest. Have a good cheese knife for guests to help themselves.

Serve with assorted crackers.

1 pound Jarlsberg Swiss cheese	6 ounces Port de Salut
	6 ounces French Brie
¼ pound Roquefort or blue cheese	1 small Gouda
	½ pound Cheddar

CHEESE ROSE:

4 ounces cream cheese, at room temperature	Real rose leaves, or other green leaves from the
4 drops food coloring (optional)	garden, or watercress
	1 thick level slice of head
1 fresh tomato, large and firm	lettuce or cabbage

In a small bowl, blend cheese with food coloring, until very smooth. Fill a teaspoon with cream cheese and level it by scraping against the rim of the bowl.

Dry the tomato carefully. Hold firmly, stem side down, with the fingers of one hand. Start at the top of the tomato and make a petal by scraping the cheese-filled spoon down on the tomato. Make a circle of 3 petals around the top of the tomato, refilling the spoon for each petal. Then drop down a half inch and make another circle of petals. The petals should not be under each other. Make the petals between the petals above. Continue to make rows of petals until close to the bottom of the tomato. Place the rose on the slice of head lettuce, or cabbage. So the rose won't slide, put a dot of cheese on the lettuce first. Surround the base of the rose with greens.

With practice your roses will look more real. The trick of applying the petals is in a twist of the wrist.

CHEESE-PUFF SQUARES

This is an interesting tidbit made with two different textured doughs, one a flaky pastry, and the other a choux paste. It is complicated, but you will need only about half of the choux paste for the cheese puffs. You can make dotlets or small cream puffs from the rest of the batter. Bake on a cookie sheet at 425° until puffed and golden. Fill with finely sliced chicken or fish salad to use as an appetizer. You can freeze the empty shells for future use.

FLAKY PASTRY:

2 cups flour	*1 teaspoon lemon juice*
½ teaspoon salt	*4 to 6 tablespoons ice water*
9 tablespoons sweet	
butter, cold	

Into a bowl, sift together the flour and salt. Add 3 tablespoons of the butter, working it in with your fingertips. Add the lemon juice to 4 tablespoons of water and cut the liquid into the mixture until a ball is formed. Use a little more water if needed.

On a lightly floured surface, roll this dough into a 12″ x 4″ rectangle. Have the dough facing you the long way. Dot the middle third of the dough with 3 tablespoons of butter cut in bits.

Fold the top third of the dough down and the bottom third of the dough up, making a 4″ square. Press the top edge with your rolling pin so that it seals together. Place the dough in a cellophane bag and chill for 30 minutes.

On a lightly floured board, place the dough with the open side facing you, roll again up and down to a 12″ x 4″ rectangle.

Proceed again as the first time. Dot the remaining butter in the center of Have the dough facing you the long way. Dot the middle third of the dough up. Chill again for 30 minutes.

Repeat the turning of the dough, rolling and folding and chilling for a third and fourth time. No butter is added the last two times.

While the dough is chilling the last time, preheat oven to 400° and prepare the choux paste.

CHOUX PASTE:

1 cup water
½ cup butter
¼ teaspoon salt
1 cup flour

4 eggs
¼ cup Parmesan cheese,
    freshly grated
⅛ teaspoon cayenne pepper

In a heavy saucepan, bring the water and butter to a boil. Add the salt and flour all at one time and stir the mixture vigorously until it leaves the sides of the pan. Remove from the heat.

Beat in the eggs, one at a time. The batter should be just thick enough to hold soft peaks. If too stiff, add another egg. Add the cheese and pepper to the batter.

Now remove the flaky pastry from the refrigerator and roll it very thin. Cut into 2½" squares.

Fill a pastry bag, with a plain tip, with some of the choux paste. Pipe a 1" puff in the center of each square of pastry dough.

EGG WASH AND TOPPING:

1 egg
2 tablespoons milk
¼ cup Gruyère cheese, grated

¼ cup Parmesan cheese,
    freshly grated

Lightly beat the egg with the milk. Brush the edges of the pastry squares with the egg-milk mix. Sprinkle the tops of choux puff generously with the grated cheeses.

Now bring up the four corners of the pastry and pinch them together to seal. Put the pastry squares on a baking sheet and brush them with the egg wash.

Bake in preheated oven for 20 minutes, or until they are golden brown and well puffed. Transfer to a serving platter. Serve warm. Makes about 18 pastries.

TARTLETS

Whenever you have tiny tartlets to fill, always cook or bake your fillings before placing them in baked shells. This will eliminate a lot of mess and give you more satisfactory results.

2 cups flour
½ teaspoon salt

¼ pound cold butter
3 tablespoons ice water

Preheat oven to 350°. In a bowl, blend the flour and salt. With your fingertips, rub the butter in until the mixture is crumbly. With a knife, cut the water gradually into the dry ingredients until a ball is formed.

Lightly grease or use nonstick spray on 2" muffin pans. Pinch off a small piece of dough, the size of a walnut. On a very lightly floured board, press the dough into a round with the heel of your hand. Fit the dough into the muffin tin. Continue in this manner to make 24 shells.

Bake for about 10 minutes, or until golden brown. After baking, turn the tart shells out on a cookie sheet.

CHEESE FILLING FOR TARTLETS:

2 cups cream
2 whole eggs plus 2 egg
   yolks
½ cup Swiss cheese,
   grated
½ cup Cheddar cheese,
   sharp, grated

2 teaspoons
   Worcestershire sauce
1 tablespoon vermouth
Dash of lemon dill
Salt and pepper to taste
Parsley and paprika
   for garnish

Preheat oven to 350°. Scald the cream. Beat the eggs and very gradually add the hot cream, beating constantly. Stir in the grated cheeses and the rest of the ingredients.

Pour the mixture into two 9″ pie pans. Set them in a larger pan of water and bake for about 20 minutes, or until a knife placed in the center of the baked filling comes out clean. Fill each tart shell with a heaping teaspoonful of cheese custard. Garnish with sprinkle of paprika and tiny sprig of parsley.

The tartlets should be served warm, so for later serving, heat them briefly in the oven.

CREAM-CHEESE PASTRY SHELLS

This amount will make 16 small tarts or barquette shells. For barquettes, use an oval-shaped pan, crimped or plain. The size for this recipe should be 4¼″ x 4¾″.

½ cup sweet butter,
  at room temperature
½ cup cream cheese,
  at room temperature

½ teaspoon salt
1 cup flour

Blend all the ingredients. Form into a ball and chill for about 3 hours.

Roll out the dough to ⅛″ thickness. Cut with the barquette or tart shell you are using, or you can bake in any small tart shells, cutting dough and then pressing into the shell. Prick the bottom of the tart with a fork. Chill for 1 hour.

Preheat oven to 400°. Bake the shells on the lowest rack of the oven for 15 minutes, or until they are puffed and golden.

FILLING FOR CHEESE BARQUETTES OR TARTS:

3 egg yolks
2 tablespoons Parmesan
  cheese, freshly grated
1 tablespoon flour
5 tablespoons heavy
  cream
1 tablespoon Gruyère-
  style cheese, grated

1 tablespoon butter
½ teaspoon Dijon
  mustard
Pinch of sugar
Salt and white pepper to taste
Dash of cayenne pepper
2 egg whites

In a saucepan, whisk together the egg yolks, Parmesan cheese and flour. Cook over low heat, stirring until thick, add the cream and continue to cook

106

and stir until the mixture is the consistency of heavy cream. Remove from the heat and stir in the Gruyère cheese, butter, mustard and seasonings. Transfer to a bowl, cover and cool.

Beat the egg whites until stiff. Fold carefully into the cheese mixture. Fill pastry shells.

MY "FRENCH BOUQUET"

The idea of this is to create a colorful combination of edibles which when completed will be a great conversational centerpiece. I'll give you some ideas, but you can use any combination of tasty tidbits that tempt the palate. You will be pleased with the realistic effect you can achieve.

1 round bread, the largest you can find
1 pound cream cheese, at room temperature
12 crab legs, marinated
12 shrimp, glazed (see page 82)
½ pound smoked salmon, or lox
½ cup salted cashews, chopped
2 4-ounce jars marinated artichoke hearts

1 small can black olives
1 jar stuffed green olives
1 small jar pickled herring filets
1 can rolled anchovy filets
½ pound Swiss cheese, in cubes
½ pound Cheddar cheese, in cubes
Carrots and celery ribs
1 bunch radishes

You will also need:

> box of round toothpicks   small fresh flowers and
> 4 10" or 12" doilies   greens (baby's-breath
>   are effective)
>   bunch of watercress

Take off all the crust of the bread, except on the bottom. Spread the bread with softened cream cheese.

Prepare the several items that you will insert into the bread on toothpicks. Put the crab legs and shrimp on toothpicks. Spread slices of smoked salmon with a little cream cheese and roll up. Slice in bite-size pieces and put each piece on a toothpick. Make tiny rolls of cream cheese and roll in chopped nuts.

Drain the artichoke hearts and the olives. Cut herring filets into bite-size pieces. Drain the anchovies. Insert toothpicks in each item. Put cheese cubes on toothpicks.

Use a vegetable peeler to run lengthwise down a carrot. Do the same with tender celery ribs. Wind strips around your forefinger and secure with a toothpick. Place in ice water. (They will be crisp and curled when you're ready to use them; just remove the toothpicks.) Make radish roses and put them in ice water.

Proceed to assemble your bouquet by sticking all the foods into the bread. Plant the foods in a scattered arrangement. Do not push the toothpicks too far down; they should be easily removed by guests.

Use fresh flowers and greens for effect. Watercress and baby's-breath and small blossoms should be tucked in among the toothpicks.

Place the bouquet on a serving platter. Cut out the center of 4 doilies, leaving an approximately 2½"-wide outer edge on each. Fold this as to pleat.

Open and place as a collar around the base of the bouquet. Place some of the vegetable curls and greens around the bouquet. Serve with bowls of My Special Mustard or Ravigote Sauce (see below), Mayonnaise (page 33) or whatever other condiment you like.

MY SPECIAL MUSTARD

This is a very snappy and delightful mustard to use with meats, fish and seafoods.

1 4-ounce can dry	*1 teaspoon salt*
mustard	*¼ pound butter*
1 cup tarragon vinegar	*6 large eggs*
½ cup sugar	*Juice of 1 lemon*

Put the mustard in a mixing bowl. Pour the vinegar over it, but do not mix. Cover and let stand overnight.

The next day, put the mustard mixture in the top of a double boiler on medium heat. Add the sugar, salt and butter. Add the eggs, one at a time, stirring constantly with a wire whisk, being careful not to let mixture curdle. Cook for 5 minutes. Remove from the heat. Add the lemon juice. Chill. In covered containers and refrigerated, the mustard will keep for several months.

RAVIGOTE SAUCE

This is a delightful dip for cold shrimp, lobster chunks or crab legs.

1 cup heavy cream,
whipped
1 cup mayonnaise
½ cup chili sauce
1 teaspoon green pepper,
finely chopped
1 teaspoon pearl onion or
scallion, finely chopped
1 teaspoon pickled beets,
finely chopped

2 eggs, hard-cooked
and chopped
1 teaspoon tarragon
vinegar
1 teaspoon ketchup
1 teaspoon lemon juice
Salt and pepper to taste
Paprika

Blend all the ingredients, and chill before serving.

OLD-FASHIONED BUFFET SUPPER

Suggestions for a complete buffet table for a party of 20 to 25 people. This is an old stand-by buffet. It's easy to do, but people really love it.

Assorted Cold Cuts and
  Cheese Platter
Horseradish Ring Filled
  with Shrimp
  Salad (see page 80)
Potato Salad en Gelée
  (see page 14)

Assorted breads
Blueberry- or strawberry-
  topped cheese cake
Assorted tray of small
  cakes
Beverages

ASSORTED COLD CUTS AND CHEESE PLATTER

1 pound sliced roast beef
1 pound sliced turkey
1 pound sliced corned
  beef
½ pound sliced pastrami
½ pound sliced ham
1 pound sliced Swiss
  cheese
Large lettuce leaves

1 green pepper
3 #2½ cans pickled
  beet buds, drained
1 jar small pickled onions
1 jar green olives,
  pitted or stuffed
1 can black olives, pitted
Parsley
6 dill pickles

Arrange the meats and cheese in neat rows on a large platter covered with lettuce leaves. Fold each slice of roast beef in half. Overlap slices in a row down one side of the platter. Place turkey slices next, then a row of Swiss cheese. Follow with a row of corned beef. Then use more roast beef and again the cheese. Roll the pastrami and ham in fingerlengths; make a little

111

stack of each. Slice the green pepper in rings. Put a ring around each stack of rolled meat. Space these around the platter.

Garnish the platter with kabobs made of beet buds, onions, olives green and black, on 4″ wooden skewers. Put dill pickles sliced lengthwise on a side plate. Serve with a basket of dark thin-sliced breads.

This Beet-and-Prune Relish is also a good accompaniment.

BEET-AND-PRUNE RELISH

1 #2 can pickled
   julienne beets
2 teaspoons cornstarch
1 teaspoon sugar
Juice of 1 lemon

1 tablespoon concentrated
   frozen orange juice
6 dried prunes, soaked,
   pitted and coarsely diced

Drain beets; set aside. Pour the juice into a saucepan and add the rest of the ingredients. Stir and cook until thickened.

Pour the sauce over the beets. Serve chilled.

PHEASANT PIE

Use a thin wheel of bread, cut from the widest part of a huge round bread, to give you a unique way to present an appetizer which is really like a pie-full of delights.

1 very large round
   dark bread
8 ounces cream cheese,
   at room temperature
Few drops green
   vegetable coloring
   (optional)
8 ounces black salmon
   eggs (or caviar if
   you're rich)

4 ounces smoked salmon,
   sliced
6 eggs, hard-cooked
1 tablespoon mayonnaise
1 teaspoon lemon juice
1 tube anchovy paste
¼ cup minced parsley

Cut a thin slice from the center of the bread all the way across to get as large a round wheel as possible. This will be a base on which to build your rings of food. Remove the crust. Assuming that your bread is 12″ in diameter, you proceed to cover it as follows (if the bread is smaller, eliminate some rings):

Divide the cream cheese in half. Tint half of it with green coloring. Spread the round of bread with the white cream cheese, covering the surface and side edge. In the center, make a 3″ round mound of caviar.

Cut the salmon in ½″ strips, then put a ring of salmon around the caviar.

Slice the eggs with an egg slicer. Put aside the white slices. Mash the yolks with the mayonnaise and lemon juice. Put this in a pastry bag with a star tube. Squeeze a ring of yolk around the salmon.

Place strips of the sliced egg whites around the yellow ring. Around the egg whites, squeeze a strip of anchovy paste.

Put the green-colored cream cheese in a pastry bag with a star tube and pipe around anchovy paste.

Repeat a ring of smoked salmon.

Make a ring of caviar. This is most easily done by putting caviar into a small cone made of parchment paper, or use a pastry bag with a small tube. Pipe with a ring of white cream cheese around the caviar ring.

At this point your bread should be completely covered. Press minced parsley around the edge of the bread. The cream cheese will hold the parsley trim on well.

Transfer the whole pie to a serving platter. Using a very sharp knife, carefully cut the pie in half; then, keeping the knife clean so the rings will not smudge, carefully cut into quarters and again into eighths. If the pie is large enough, cut again into sixteenths. Keep the pie intact.

Have a small pie server or silver knife near the platter so guests can help themselves to a wedge of "Pheasant Pie."

QUICK PICK-UPS

Spread flat side of large pecan halves with mashed Roquefort cheese. Put the two halves together.

Using a pastry bag with a small round tube, stuff pitted large green olives with a mixture of cream cheese, black caviar and dash of onion juice.

Soak large pitted dates in brandy for several hours. Drain and fill with cream cheese to which you've added ¼ teaspoon horseradish. Place in paper candy cups to serve.

Drain canned artichoke bottoms. Fill with black caviar. Top with dab of sour cream and sprinkle with chopped chives. Place on toast rounds if you wish.

Spread thin sliced ham with cream cheese and My Special Mustard (see page 109). Roll and secure with frilled toothpick.

Spread thin slice of rare roast beef with My Special Mustard (see page 109). Roll around a spike of dill pickle. Secure with colored toothpick.

REUBEN SANDWICH

Before coming to Portland, I visited Reuben's in New York and I ordered their famous sandwich. I really enjoyed it, but for my restaurant, I concocted my own version. The sandwich became so popular that many local eating establishments began featuring a "Reuben," but no one equaled ours.

This is a "he-man" sandwich that is very filling for a meal, or divided, can serve as a snack.

2 pounds rye or pumpernickel bread, thinly sliced

For one sandwich:

3 of largest slices from loaf of bread
3 ounces Swiss cheese, sliced
3 ounces corned beef, sliced

2 ounces sauerkraut, drained
3 ounces turkey, sliced
2 tablespoons butter, melted
Dill pickles and cherry tomatoes for garnish

Put half of the Swiss cheese on one slice of bread. Cover the cheese with the corned beef, then half of the sauerkraut. Add the second slice of bread. Cover it with the turkey, then the rest of the sauerkraut and Swiss cheese. Top with the third slice of bread and brush it with melted butter.

Place the sandwich, buttered side down, on a preheated grill, then spread butter on the top side. When it is brown and the cheese has melted, use a large spatula to turn over and grill the other side.

When ready, remove the sandwich with spatula to a cutting board. Insert toothpicks to hold sandwich together and cut into thirds or fourths, as desired. Serve on a large plate with garnish.

GARNISH SUGGESTIONS

AS A CENTERPIECE FOR A CHEESE TRAY:

Using a large Gouda or Edam cheese, scoop out balls of cheese with a melon baller. Stick a frilled toothpick in each small ball, and replace them in the large cheese.

TO ADD COLORFUL TOUCH TO COLD PLATTERS OF FOOD:

Garnish with small skewers of vegetable combinations, such as cherry tomatoes, pickled onions, black and green olives, gherkins, baby beets, chunked dill pickles or any zesty small vegetables at hand.

Also use skewered fresh-fruit combinations, such as assorted melon balls in season, orange and grapefruit sections, grapes, bing cherries, or balls of fresh pineapple and papaya.

FOR AN ATTRACTIVE CENTERPIECE:

Blanch a large head of cauliflower for 2 or 3 minutes in salted boiling water. Drain. Place on a bed of greens. With toothpicks, stick a variety of vegetables into the cauliflower. Choose from cherry tomatoes, carrot curls, black and green olives, artichoke hearts, fresh asparagus tips, radish roses and sticks of green and red pepper. Sprigs of watercress stuck here and there are a nice touch.

TO SHAPE HARD-COOKED EGGS INTO "APPLES":

Cover the eggs with cold water in a saucepan, bring to a rolling boil, uncovered. Turn off the heat and let the eggs remain in the pan for about 10 minutes. Then cool the eggs under running water.

Shell the eggs. Take each egg and hold it between the palms of your hands. Press the ends of the eggs tightly toward each other to form an apple!

Put a whole clove into blossom end. Insert reverse clove with stem up on the bottom side. Sprinkle liberally with paprika.

These egg "apples" make a nice garnish on a platter of cold cuts and cheeses.

117

LEMON BASKET—AN ATTRACTIVE GARNISH FOR FISH PLATTERS:

With a sharp paring knife, cut around the middle of a lemon zigzag fashion. Pull apart to separate halves. Take slice from bottom of each half so basket sits level. Stick a few sprigs of watercress in the center of each lemon basket and place a rose on it.

CHEDDAR-CHEESE CARROT AND CRABAPPLE:

8 ounces Cheddar cheese,	*Whole cloves*
at room temperature	*Paprika*
Parsley	

Mash the cheese until soft. Use 1 scant tablespoon of cheese to make a ball, rolling in the palm of your hands. Elongate the ball into carrot shape. Stick a parsley stem on the top of the carrot. Sprinkle with paprika.

Roll the cheese into a ball the size of a walnut. Put a whole clove, blossom side out, on the bottom of the apple. Use the green stem from parsley on top of the apple. Sprinkle with paprika.

SPRAY OF RADISHES:

I like this garnish on a vegetable or meat platter. It's a little conversation piece, simple but attractive.

1 large bunch green	*1 bunch of radishes*
onions	

Clean the onions but keep them intact with green stems. Retie the scallions into a bunch. Clean the radishes and remove the stems. Insert a toothpick from the base of the onion far enough so pick will hold a radish on the top of each onion.

Glaze:

½ tablespoon plain
  gelatin
2 tablespoons cold water
2 tablespoons boiling
  water

Juice of 1 lemon
½ teaspoon salt

Mix gelatin and cold water and let stand until absorbed. Dissolve with the boiling water. Add the lemon juice and salt. Chill slightly.

Spoon the glaze over the radishes. Refrigerate the bunch until set. Glaze the radishes again. Chill until ready to use your bouquet.

CAVIAR TOWERS

A bit tedious to do, but attractive and tasty. We haven't listed amounts for the ingredients. They will depend on the size of your bread.

Cream cheese
Black caviar
Grated onion
Egg yolks, hard-cooked

Russian salad dressing
Pickled onions, cocktail size
Pimento, for garnish
Rye bread, sliced very thin

119

Cut bread into rounds of 3″, 2″ and 1″ in diameter. Spread layer of caviar that has been seasoned with grated onion.

Top the caviar with the next smaller size round of bread that has already been spread with mashed egg yolk blended with a little Russian dressing.

Cover the smallest round of bread with cream cheese put through a pastry bag with star tube. Place it on the egg layer.

Top the "tower" with an onion and garnish with pimento.

SAUTÉED LIVERS WITH APPLE

Liver and apples? They're very good together, as you'll see.

Small red apples	Salt and pepper
Butter	3″ toast rounds
Chicken livers	

Core the apples and slice crosswise ¼″ thick. Sauté in butter until almost tender. Season the livers and sauté.

Place an apple slice on each round of toast. Top with a liver. Hold the liver in place with a cocktail pick.

WAFFLED BEEF AND CHEESE

Rye bread, thinly sliced,　　　　*Corned beef, thinly sliced*
　　cut into squares or　　　　*Swiss cheese, thinly sliced*
　　rounds　　　　　　　　　　*Softened butter*
Mustard　　　　　　　　　　　*Dill pickles*

Preheat the waffle iron. Spread the bread with mustard. Put a layer of meat and cheese between two pieces of bread. Brush outsides of the sandwich with butter.

Place four sandwiches at a time, or more, if your waffle iron can accommodate them, in a waffle iron and toast golden brown.

Serve with dill pickle.

ANCHOVY CANAPÉ

3" rounds of rye bread　　　　*Lemon juice*
Anchovy paste　　　　　　　*Anchovy filets*
Fresh mushrooms,　　　　　　*Chives, minced*
　　thinly sliced

Spread bread rounds with a layer of anchovy paste. Add a layer of mushrooms that have been marinated in lemon juice.

Place an anchovy filet on top. Sprinkle with chives.

121

🌹

TOASTED HAM ROLLS

10 slices white bread
½ pound boiled ham,
   lean thin slices

3 ounces cream cheese
4 tablespoons sweet pickle
   relish, drained

Decrust the bread. Flatten each slice with a rolling pin. Cover slice with a thin layer of ham.

Blend the cream cheese and pickle relish. Spread a thin layer over the ham. Roll up tightly and toast on all sides on a grill.

To use as a canapé, cut each roll into two or three segments. Secure each piece with a cocktail pick.

🌹

ARTICHOKE CANAPÉ

Rounds of bread
Butter, at room
   temperature
Small canned whole
   artichoke hearts, split
   in half

Lobster or crabmeat
Mayonnaise
Tabasco sauce
Parmesan cheese, grated

Butter bread rounds. Put half an artichoke heart on each piece.

122

Mash seafood with a little mayonnaise and a dash of Tabasco sauce. Put ½ teaspoonful of the mixture in the center of the artichoke. Sprinkle with cheese. Put under the broiler until the cheese melts.

SHRIMP DIP

16 ounces small shrimp, cooked	1 teaspoon Worcestershire sauce
1 cup sour cream	½ teaspoon curry powder
6 ounces cream cheese	8 pitted black olives
Juice of 1 lemon	2 tablespoons dry sherry

Combine all the ingredients in a blender. Whirl for 1 minute. Serve with potato chips.

ANCHOVY DIP

8 ounces cream cheese, at room temperature	1 2-ounce tube anchovy paste
1 2¼-ounce jar of capers in vinegar	¼ cup beer

Blend all the ingredients with a whisk until smooth. Thin with more beer if desired. Serve with potato chips and crisp corn chips.

AVOCADO TOMATO DIP

2 avocados, well ripened
2 tablespoons lemon juice
2 tablespoons vinegar
1 tomato, peeled
¼ cup onion
½ teaspoon sugar

2 teaspoons salt
1 teaspoon
   Worcestershire sauce
⅛ teaspoon pepper
4 dashes Tabasco sauce

Peel and pit avocados, then purée in a blender with the lemon juice and vinegar. Mix in the tomato and onion. Add seasonings.

   Cover tightly and chill. Serve as a dip for fresh or spiced vegetables.

HOT CHILI DIP

This is very tasty.

1 pound lean ground beef
1 cup chili sauce
1½ tablespoons chili
   powder

1 package dehydrated
   onion-mushroom soup*
2 cups sour cream

* If not available, use ½ package onion, ½ mushroom soup.

In a skillet, stir and brown the beef. Drain off any grease. Mix in the rest of the ingredients. Heat thoroughly, but do not let boil.

Serve with taco or other corn-type chips.

SMOKED SALMON AND CUCUMBER DIP

*2 medium-size
   cucumbers, peeled
1 cup sour cream
3 tablespoons vinegar
1½ teaspoons chives,
   minced
1 teaspoon dill weed*

*1 teaspoon salt
Dash of white pepper
Dash of Tabasco sauce
½ pound smoked salmon,
   in bite-size squares
Fresh dill for garnish*

Scoop seeds out of the cucumber and dice. Whirl in a blender with all the ingredients except the smoked salmon. Pour into a serving bowl and place it in the center of a large platter. Surround the bowl with the pieces of smoked salmon and garnish with fresh dill.

Use little cocktail forks for dipping. Serve with thinly sliced pumpernickel.

ORANGE EGGNOG

This is one of the eggnog variations that I have found were well acclaimed.

2 quarts milk
12 eggs, separated
1½ cups sugar
2 teaspoons vanilla

1 6-ounce can frozen
   orange juice concentrate,
   thawed
1 cup orange liqueur
Orange sections for garnish

Scald the milk. Beat the egg yolks with 1 cup of the sugar, add 1 cup of the hot milk, then quickly blend in the egg mixture. Place on low heat and stir constantly until the mixture thickens and coats a metal spoon. Remove from the heat and transfer to a large bowl. Pour in the remaining milk and the vanilla. Chill. Add the orange juice concentrate.

Pour into a punch bowl with the liqueur. Top with meringue floats. Garnish with orange sections.

MERINGUE FLOATS FOR ORANGE EGGNOG:

Beat the egg whites until foamy. Add remaining ½ cup of sugar, 2 tablespoons at a time. Continue beating until the mixture stands in stiff peaks.

Float dollops of meringue in the punch bowl and place some meringue on each serving of eggnog.

126

HEIRLOOM EGGNOG

12 eggs, separated
1 cup sugar
2 cups light rum or
   brandy, or a
   combination of both

1 quart milk
2 teaspoons vanilla
1 quart heavy cream
Dash of nutmeg

Beat the egg yolks until light. Add the sugar, and continue beating until the sugar is dissolved. Beat in the liquor, then the milk and vanilla. Chill for several hours or overnight.

Just before serving, beat the egg whites until stiff but not dry. Whip the cream. Fold the whites and cream into the yolk mixture. Pour into a punch bowl. Sprinkle with nutmeg.

COFFEE EGGNOG

6 eggs, separated
2 cups half-and-half
   cream
2 cups milk
¾ cup sugar
1 cup brandy

2 cups light rum
3 cups strong coffee
Dash of salt
1 cup heavy cream
Nutmeg

127

Beat the egg yolks until thick and lemon-colored. Blend in the cream, milk, sugar, brandy, rum, coffee and a dash of salt.

Beat the egg whites until stiff but not dry. Whip the cream. Fold the whites and cream into the eggnog. Pour into a punch bowl. Sprinkle with nutmeg.

SNAPPY BLOODY MARYS & CRISP CELERY STICKS

4 cups tomato juice
1 cup vodka
1 tablespoon
  Worcestershire sauce
2 teaspoons horseradish

1 tablespoon fresh lime
  juice
1 teaspoon Tabasco sauce
Dash of salt

Put all the ingredients in a blender and mix. Chill well. Serve in ice-filled glasses.

CELERY STICKS:

Cut a bunch of celery hearts into 3″ sticks. Crisp in ice water. Drain before serving. Sprinkle with celery salt and pepper.

SMALL CAKES,
COOKIES
&
DESSERTS

VIENNESE ALMOND PINKS

Here's an outstanding cookie that's very popular with everyone. This recipe will provide a large batch, but these cookies freeze and keep very well.

½ pound butter	1 teaspoon vanilla
½ cup powdered sugar	2½ cups flour
½ cup granulated sugar	¼ teaspoon salt
3 egg yolks	1½ cups red-raspberry jam

Preheat oven to 350°. Grease and flour a 12″ x 18″ jelly-roll pan. Cream the butter and sugars until fluffy. Add the egg yolks and vanilla. Blend in the flour and salt. Flour your hand and press the dough evenly on the bottom of the pan.

Bake until golden, for about 20 minutes. Remove from the oven. Spread with the jam. Cover with almond filling.

ALMOND FILLING:

1½ pounds almond paste*	2 cups sugar
10 eggs	2 teaspoons vanilla
¾ pound sweet butter	1 cup flour
	¼ teaspoon salt

* You can buy the almond paste at the supermarket.

In a blender or food processor, whirl chunks of the almond paste with the eggs. Do about a third of the amount at a time. Make sure this mixture is smooth.

In a large bowl, cream the butter, add the sugar. Blend in the almond mixture, then the vanilla, flour and salt. Beat until the batter is very smooth. Pour this over the jam-covered cookie crust.

Bake for about 35 minutes, or until the center feels quite firm to the touch. Remove from the oven and let cool in the pan.

ICING AND TOPPING:

2 cups powdered sugar
½ cup grenadine or
  maraschino cherry
  juice
2 teaspoons corn syrup

2 tablespoons sweet butter,
  at room temperature
½ cup pistachio nuts,*
  finely ground

Beat all the ingredients except the nuts together and spread carefully over the baked cookie. Sprinkle the nuts over the icing. When it is completely set, use a sharp knife to cut the cookie into 1½" x ¾" strips.

* If you can't get pistachios, use ground blanched almonds. Shake them in a jar with a few drops of green food coloring to tint.

APPLE FLUFF

This is a simple, refreshing dessert.

3 cups water	*6 Golden Delicious apples,*
2 cups plus 3 tablespoons	* peeled, cored and sliced*
* sugar*	*1 cup heavy cream*
Rind of 1 small lemon	*2 tablespoons rum*

In a saucepan, combine the water, 2 cups of the sugar and lemon rind. Bring to a boil. Remove crystals from the sides of the pan with a brush dipped in cold water. Boil the syrup for 5 minutes.

Add the apple slices and cook until tender. Remove the apples and purée. Chill.

Whip the cream, adding the remaining sugar and the rum, until it holds soft peaks. Fold the apple purée into the cream. Pour into individual dessert bowls or sherbet glasses.

APPLE PASTRY

This cream-cheese dough makes a tender and light pastry.

FILLING:

6 large tart apples, cut in pieces ¾ cup sugar	3 teaspoons cinnamon 2 teaspoons vanilla 2 lemons, juice and grated peel

In a 2-quart saucepan, put the apple pieces. Cover and cook on medium heat until the apples are soft. Remove from the heat and press the apples through a strainer. Add the sugar and flavorings. Set aside to cool completely.

If, after straining, the apple mixture seems too thin, add a tablespoon of cornstarch mixed with lemon juice. Return to the heat and stir constantly until thickened, then set aside to cool.

PASTRY DOUGH:

2 cups sweet butter,
   at room temperature
1 pound cream cheese,
   at room temperature
	5½ cups flour
	½ teaspoon salt

Preheat oven to 375°. Lightly grease a cookie sheet. In a large bowl, cream the butter and cream cheese until fluffy. Add the flour and salt. Mix until well combined. Wrap and chill for at least 2 hours.

When thoroughly chilled, cut the dough into eight pieces. Use one piece at a time, leaving the balance of dough refrigerated.

Roll the piece of dough into a ⅛"-thick circle; cut into eight or nine pie-shaped wedges and place a tablespoon of apple filling on each wedge. Roll from the wide side to the point. Place on the cookie sheet and bake for 20 to 25 minutes, or until golden brown. Sprinkle with powdered sugar. Repeat the procedure with the remaining pieces of dough. This recipe makes about 6 dozen pastries, and they freeze well.

FRENCH APPLE SQUARES

These are very delightful. They taste like a special apple pie, but the crust is a rich cookie dough.

CRUST:

4½ cups flour	4 egg yolks
1 teaspoon salt	2 tablespoons lemon juice
⅓ cup sugar	2 tablespoons rum
1 cup sweet butter, chilled	⅔ cup sour cream

Preheat oven to 450°. Lightly grease and flour a jelly-roll pan 15" x 11" x 1½".
Into a large bowl, sift the flour, salt and sugar. With your fingertips, blend
in the butter until the mixture is crumbly. Work the eggs, juice, rum and
cream into the mixture by cutting in with knife or heavy spatula until a
ball of dough is formed.

Turn the dough onto a lightly floured board. Knead for 1 minute. Cut off
two thirds of the dough. Refrigerate the other piece.

Roll the larger piece of dough into a rectangle ¼"-thick and a little larger
than the bottom surface of the baking pan. Drape the dough around the rolling
pin and transfer it to the prepared pan. The dough should line the bottom
and the sides of the pan. Prick the dough with a fork. Bake for 10 to 15
minutes, or until lightly browned. Place on a rack to cool. Reduce oven heat
to 350°.

FILLING:

6 tablespoons sweet
  butter
1½ cups sugar
½ cup light-brown
  sugar
4 tablespoons frozen
  concentrated orange
  juice
4 tablespoons lemon juice

Grated rind of 2 oranges
12 tart apples, peeled,
  cored and thickly sliced
1 egg, beaten
½ cup sugar mixed with
  2 tablespoons cinnamon
1 cup almonds, blanched
  and slivered

In a heavy skillet, combine butter, sugars, juices and orange rind. Cook
over low heat, stirring until the sugar is dissolved.

136

Add the prepared apples to the sauce and cook only partially, for about 5 minutes. With a slotted spoon, remove the apple slices. Continue to simmer the sauce until it thickens. Arrange the apples in rows on the baked crust. Spoon the thickened sauce over the apples.

Roll out the balance of the dough in a rectangle large enough to cover the pan. Drape the dough around the rolling pin and unroll it over the apples. Brush the dough with the egg. Sprinkle with the cinnamon-sugar mixture and then with the almonds.

Bake for about 25 minutes, or until the top crust is lightly brown. Let cool. Cut into 2″ squares.

BOHEMIAN COOKIE

This cookie dough is an excellent basic dough that can be used in several ways, shown below.

3 egg yolks, hard-cooked
4 tablespoons cream
2 tablespoons orange
rind, grated
2 tablespoons lemon
rind, grated
1 tablespoon vanilla

1 pound sweet butter,
at room temperature
1 cup powdered sugar
1 cup granulated sugar
3 raw egg yolks
5 cups flour
1 teaspoon salt

Preheat oven to 350°. To hard-boil the eggs: Place 3 eggs in a saucepan, cover with cold water, bring to a rolling boil, uncovered. Turn off the heat, let the eggs stay in the water for 10 minutes, then cool under running water. Shell and remove the yolks.

Mash the egg yolks through a sieve. Add the cream and flavorings. Set aside.

In a large bowl, cream the butter and add the sugars. Blend in the yolk mixture, the raw yolks and the flour sifted with the salt.

Proceed to form cookies: Put dough in a pastry bag with large star tip and press onto a cookie sheet, or use a cookie press with plates for various shapes.

Bake for 10 to 12 minutes, or until golden brown. These cookies will remain crisp in airtight cans or properly wrapped and frozen.

Various ways of using the dough:

Roll the dough into small balls. Dip in fluffed egg white and then press into the mixture of cinnamon and sugar.

Bake on a cookie sheet in preheated oven as above.

Add melted semisweet chocolate to some of the dough for chocolate cookies.

Combine white and chocolate dough in a pastry bag for a swirl effect.

Roll a piece of white dough, then roll a piece of chocolate dough. Place on top of each other. Roll up and slice for pinwheel effect.

This dough can be pressed in a jelly-roll pan as the bottom crust for the Viennese Almond Pinks (see page 131).

This dough can be pressed into a spring-form pan as crust for a cheese cake. Bohemian dough, when used as a crust, is also known as *Mürbteig*.

BROWNIE WITH CHEESE SWIRL

This recipe makes a large batch of a rich brownie. Even reading it may make you want to try a half recipe, or freeze some.

BROWNIE:

8 squares unsweetened
   baking chocolate
2 cups sweet butter
4 cups sugar
8 eggs, large

1 teaspoon vanilla
3 cups flour
½ teaspoon salt
2 cups pecans, coarsely
   chopped

Preheat oven to 350°. Grease a 15" x 10" x 2" baking pan. In a large pie pan, place the chocolate and butter in the oven to melt. Let cool.

In a large bowl, combine the chocolate-and-butter mixture with the sugar, eggs and vanilla. Blend in the flour sifted with the salt. Stir in the pecans. The dough will be semifirm.

Spread half of the dough in the prepared pan and bake for 30 minutes, or until firm. Remove from the oven and spread with the filling:

FILLING:

1 pound cream cheese,
   at room temperature
½ cup sugar

1 teaspoon cinnamon
2 teaspoons vanilla
2 tablespoons sour cream

Blend all the ingredients until smooth. Spread over the baked layer. Cover the filling with the balance of the brownie dough. With a knife, gently swirl through the filling and top layer.

Bake for 50 to 60 minutes, or until a wooden pick, put into the middle of the pan, comes out clean. Let cool thoroughly, and thinly ice with chocolate frosting:

FROSTING:

6 squares semisweet chocolate

4 tablespoons sweet butter
2 tablespoons corn syrup

Melt together. Stir until smooth. Spread over the brownies. When the frosting is set, cut the brownies into small squares or bars.

A "SPECIAL" BROWNIE

This is a brownie with a different twist. It has a meringue topping, is very moist and retains its freshness for some time. It's a sinful treat!

4 ounces unsweetened chocolate
1 cup sweet butter, at room temperature
1½ cups sugar
1 tablespoon vanilla

4 eggs
1 cup flour
½ teaspoon salt
½ teaspoon baking powder
2 cups pecans, coarsely chopped

Preheat oven to 325°. Grease a 10″ x 15″ x 3″ baking pan. Melt the chocolate and set aside to cool. Cream the butter. Blend in the sugar and vanilla. Beat until fluffy. Beat in the eggs, then stir in the slightly cooled chocolate.

Sift together the flour, salt and baking powder. Stir these dry ingredients into the batter. Add the nuts and blend well. Pour into the pan.

MERINGUE TOPPING:

2 extra large egg whites
½ cup sugar
1 teaspoon vanilla

2 cups miniature
marshmallows

Beat the egg whites until stiff, but not dry. Gradually beat in the sugar, a tablespoon at a time, until you have a stiff meringue. Blend in the vanilla and fold in the marshmallows

Spread the meringue over the brownie batter. Gently run a knife through the topping and into the top of the batter to create a slightly marbleized effect. Bake for about 45 minutes, or until the meringue is delicately golden.

Let cool, then run a knife around the sides of pan to loosen. Use a sharp knife to cut the brownies in about 2″ squares.

ROSE'S ORIGINAL CHEESE CAKE

This cheese cake was always *the* favorite with our customers.

CRUMB CRUST:

3 tablespoons sweet butter,
   at room temperature
1½ cups graham-cracker
   crumbs

¼ cup brown sugar
1 tablespoon cinnamon

Preheat oven to 400°. Use butter to grease a 15" x 10" x 1" jelly-roll pan. Mix the rest of the ingredients and press on the bottom and sides of the pan.

CHEESE CAKE:

6 eggs, separated
¾ cup sugar
1 cup heavy cream
1¼ pounds cream cheese,
   at room temperature

Scant ½ cup flour
2 ounces sweet butter,
   at room temperature
1 tablespoon vanilla

Preheat oven to 400°.

Beat the egg whites until foamy. Gradually add ¼ cup of sugar, a tablespoon at a time, beating constantly until the whites are stiff. Set aside.

Whip the cream until thick. Set aside.

142

In a large bowl, beat the cream cheese until fluffy. Blend in 1 cup of sugar. Add the egg yolks, two at a time, beating constantly until all yolks have been added. Add the flour, butter and vanilla. Fold in whipped cream and lastly fold in egg whites.

Pour the batter into the crust. Bake in 400° oven for 10 minutes, reduce the heat to 350° and bake for about 1 hour, or until the center of the cake feels quite solid.

Let the cake cool in the pan. When cold, cut into 2″ squares. Sprinkle with powdered sugar, or use a fruit topping (see page 148).

To serve, place each square in a paper candy cup. Yields 3 dozen.

DOUBLE CHOCOLATE CHEESE CAKE

This goodie is wonderful for chocolate addicts.

CHOCOLATE CRUST:

4 tablespoons sweet butter,
at room temperature
1½ cups chocolate wafers,
finely crushed

¼ cup sugar
¼ teaspoon cinnamon

Preheat oven to 350°. Grease a 10″ x 15″ x 2″ jelly-roll pan with the softened butter.

Combine the chocolate crumbs, sugar and cinnamon. Press the mixture evenly on the bottom and sides of the pan.

CHOCOLATE CHEESE FILLING:

1 pound cream cheese   *2 teaspoons vanilla*
1½ cups sugar   *4 eggs*
6 tablespoons Dutch cocoa *4 cups sour cream*

With an electric beater, whip the cream cheese until fluffy. Gradually add the sugar, cocoa and vanilla. Blend in the eggs, one at a time. Add the sour cream and mix thoroughly.

Pour the batter into the pan. Should the batter come to the top of the pan, make a foil collar and tie it around the pan with a string. Bake for about 45 to 50 minutes, or until the edge of the cake is set.

Chill the cake thoroughly. Cut into 2" squares.

TOPPING:

1 cup heavy cream   *2-ounce chunk of*
½ cup sugar   *milk chocolate*
1 tablespoon coffee liqueur

Whip the cream until it is of good spreading consistency. Blend in the sugar and liqueur. Spread over the top of the cold cheese cake, or you can put cream in a pastry bag with a star tube and decorate each square. Use a vegetable peeler to make chocolate curls and place them decoratively on the cream.

Put each square in a paper candy cup to serve. Yields 3 dozen.

PINEAPPLE REFRIGERATOR CHEESE CAKE

This is a flavorful, easy, no-fail cheese cake.

CRUST:

1 cup graham-cracker crumbs　　*1 teaspoon cinnamon*
¼ cup sugar

Liberally butter a 15″ x 10″ x 1″ jelly-roll pan. Blend all ingredients. Press evenly into bottom of pan.

CHEESE CAKE:

1 20-ounce can crushed　　　*Dash of salt*
　pineapple　　　　　　　　*2 tablespoons lemon juice*
3 tablespoons plain gelatin　*2 tablespoons lemon rind,*
5 eggs, separated　　　　　　*grated*
1 cup sugar　　　　　　　　*½ teaspoon vinegar*
1½ cups heavy cream　　　　*2 pounds cream cheese*

Drain the pineapple but save the juice. Sprinkle gelatin into ½ cup of the pineapple juice. Let stand.

In the top of a double boiler, beat the yolks lightly. Gradually add ½ cup of the sugar, stir in ½ cup of the cream and the salt. Cook over boiling water, stirring constantly until the custard is slightly thickened and coats your spoon. Add the soaked gelatin and stir until it dissolves. Remove from the heat. Let cool. Add the lemon juice and rind.

Beat the egg whites until foamy. Add the vinegar. Continue beating while adding the remaining sugar, a tablespoon at a time, until the whites are stiff. Set aside.

Whip the remaining heavy cream until stiff. Set aside.

Beat the cream cheese and gradually blend in the cooled custard. Add the pineapple. Fold in the whipped cream and egg whites. Pour the batter into the pan. Refrigerate until set, at least 4 hours, or overnight.

To serve, cut the cake into 2″ squares. Glaze and place in paper candy cups. Yields 3 dozen.

GLAZE FOR PINEAPPLE CHEESE CAKE:

1 cup concentrated orange juice
½ cup sugar
2 tablespoons cornstarch

A little pineapple juice
2 tablespoons grenadine syrup, or maraschino-cherry juice

In a saucepan, stir the orange juice and sugar together. Bring to a boil. Dissolve the cornstarch in the pineapple juice and stir into the hot mixture. Cook while stirring until glossy and thick. Add the red juice to enhance the color of the glaze. Chill thoroughly. Put a daub of glaze on each square of cake.

146

CHEESE-CAKE SQUARES

This is an unbaked filling in a crumb crust. Top with a fruit topping of your choice (or see page 148). These are very attractive and enjoyable.

CRUST:

½ cup sweet butter,
  at room temperature
1 cup rolled oats
2 tablespoons cinnamon

½ cup blanched almonds,
  toasted and ground
½ cup light-brown sugar

Preheat oven to 350°. Grease a 10″ x 15″ x 2″ pan generously with butter. Toast the rolled oats in another flat pan, in the oven, until lightly browned. Grind in a blender or food processor.

Combine with the rest of the ingredients. Sprinkle the mixture over the pan. Press down on the bottom and sides to form an even crust.

Bake for 8 to 10 minutes. Chill before filling.

CHEESE-CAKE FILLING:

1 pound cream cheese,
  at room temperature
2 14-ounce cans
  sweetened condensed
  milk
⅔ cup fresh lemon juice

1 teaspoon vanilla
2 tablespoons orange
  liqueur
2 cups heavy cream,
  whipped

147

In a large bowl, beat the cheese until fluffy. Gradually add the canned milk and juice. Continue beating until thick and creamy. Blend in the flavorings. Fold in half of the whipped cream. Use the rest of the cream for garnish.

Pour the filling into the chilled crust. Refrigerate for several hours.

When ready to serve, cover with a fruit topping.

BLUEBERRY TOPPING:

1 10-ounce package unsweetened frozen blueberries	2 lemons, juice and grated rind
1 cup sugar	2 tablespoons cornstarch
	2 tablespoons cold water

In a saucepan, put half the frozen berries, the sugar, lemon juice and rind. Cook and stir gently until the sugar has dissolved. Mix the cornstarch and water. Gradually add to the berry mixture while stirring.

When the mixture is thickened, remove from the heat and pour over the remaining frozen berries. Blend carefully.

STRAWBERRY TOPPING:

2 10-ounce packages unsweetened frozen strawberries	3 tablespoons cornstarch
1 cup sugar	4 tablespoons cold water
	Juice of 1 lemon

Completely defrost 1 package of frozen berries. Add the sugar and cook to a rolling boil.

Dissolve the cornstarch in the water, and while stirring add it to boiling fruit mixture. Keep stirring until the mixture is thickened and glossy.

Pour over the remaining frozen berries. Add the lemon juice and blend gently. Taste for tartness.

This amount will be sufficient to cover one large cheese cake, with an extra bowl of topping for those who want more.

To serve: Cut the cake into 2″ squares. Put the remaining whipped cream in a pastry bag with a star. Press a star on top of each square. Serve in paper crinkle cups.

CHOCOLATE ALMOND SQUARES

These delicious cookies freeze very well.

DOUGH:

½ cup sweet butter,
   at room temperature
½ cup brown sugar,
   firmly packed
1 teaspoon vanilla

¼ teaspoon salt
1½ cups flour
¾ cup raspberry jam,
   seedless

Preheat oven to 350°. Grease a 13″ x 9″ x 2″ pan. Combine all the ingredients except the jam. Mix until smooth. Pat the dough evenly into the pan. Partially bake just until lightly golden, then spread with the jam.

BATTER:

3 eggs
8 ounces almond paste
½ cup sugar

1 cup blanched almonds,
    toasted and ground
1 teaspoon almond flavoring

In a blender, mix all the ingredients until smooth. Pour onto the cookie base and bake for 20 minutes, or until golden brown. Let cool before applying the icing.

TOPPING:

1 ounce unsweetened
    chocolate
2 tablespoons sweet
    butter, at room
    temperature

2 tablespoons cream
1½ cups powdered sugar
1 tablespoon Kahlúa liqueur
½ cup blanched almonds,
    toasted and ground

Melt the chocolate, add the butter, sugar, cream and liqueur. Blend well. Spread over the baked cookie. Sprinkle with the ground almonds.

When set, cut into 1½″ squares. Place in paper candy cups.

CHOCOLATE CHEWY NUT BARS

*12 ounces semisweet
  chocolate pieces*
*1 14-ounce can sweetened
  condensed milk*
*2 tablespoons sweet
  butter*
*1 cup sweet butter,
  melted*

*1 pound light-brown
  sugar*
2 eggs
1 teaspoon salt
1 cup pecans, chopped
¾ cup flaked coconut
1 teaspoon vanilla
2 cups all-purpose flour

Preheat oven to 350°. Use a 9″ x 12″ x 1½″ ungreased baking pan. Combine the chocolate, milk and the 2 tablespoons of butter in a pan. Place in the oven to melt. Set aside to cool.

In a large mixing bowl, blend the melted butter, sugar, eggs, salt, nuts, coconut, vanilla and flour. Mix well.

Spread half of the dough to cover the bottom of the pan. Cover the dough with the chocolate mixture, then cover this with the balance of the dough. Bake for 30 to 35 minutes until golden brown. Cool and cut into 1½″ squares. Place in paper candy cups.

CHOCOLATE HAYSTACKS

These are chewy and tasty. Notice that no flour is used.

4 squares unsweetened	*½ teaspoon salt*
chocolate	*4 cups coconut*
4 tablespoons butter	*1½ cups blanched almonds,*
4 eggs	*toasted and ground*
⅔ cup sugar	*2 teaspoons vanilla*

Preheat oven to 325°. Grease a cookie sheet. In a small pan, melt the chocolate with the butter in the oven. Remove from the oven and place in a large bowl. Add the eggs, sugar, salt, coconut, almonds and vanilla. Stir until smooth.

Drop from a teaspoon onto the cookie sheet. Bake for 15 minutes. With a wide spatula, remove from the pan while still warm.

Serve in paper cups. Yield: 5 dozen haystacks.

RELATIVELY LOW-CALORIE CHOCOLATE MERINGUES

Very simple but good, and only a little fattening—compared to other things.

3 egg whites
¼ teaspoon salt
¼ teaspoon white
   vinegar
1 cup sugar

6 squares unsweetened
   chocolate, melted and
   cooled
1 teaspoon vanilla

Preheat oven to 350°. Lightly grease a cookie sheet. In a small bowl, beat the whites until foamy. Add the salt and vinegar. While still beating, add the sugar, one tablespoon at a time, and continue beating until whites are stiff and glossy. Carefully fold in the chocolate and vanilla.

Place the mixture in a pastry bag with a star tube. Press out meringues on the cookie sheet. Bake for 15 minutes. Cool and put in covered cans for better keeping.

This recipe yields 36 meringues.

CHOCOLATE MOUSSE PUFFS

This pastry was especially popular at all of our autograph parties for *Sinfully Delicious* number 1.

Make one recipe of Choux Paste (page 213). Make small puffs or dotlets, or larger cream puffs or éclairs, whichever pleases you.

MOUSSE FILLING:

10 egg yolks

1½ cups sugar

½ cup water

½ teaspoon cream of
  tartar

½ teaspoon salt

1½ pounds sweet butter

1 tablespoon rum

8 tablespoons Dutch cocoa

In a large bowl, beat the egg yolks until thick and lemon-colored. Set aside.

In a medium-size saucepan, combine the sugar, water, cream of tartar and salt. Cook and keep stirring constantly until the sugar is dissolved. Wash the sides of the pan with a pastry brush dipped in cold water to remove any sugar crystals. Continue cooking until a fork dipped in the syrup and held high spins a long thread.

Slowly pour the syrup into the yolks while beating constantly; then, still beating, gradually add the butter in bits until the mixture is thick. Blend in the rum and cocoa.

When the puffs are baked and cooled, cut a little cap off the top and fill them with the mousse. For dotlets, this is most easily done with a pastry bag with a small round tube; for larger puffs you can fill with spoonfuls. (This mixture keeps very well under refrigeration or can be frozen.) When filled, replace caps of puffs and frost.

CHOCOLATE ICING:

8 ounces semisweet
  chocolate

4 ounces sweet butter

1 teaspoon vanilla

Melt the chocolate with the butter. Cool and add vanilla. Stir until smooth. Spoon a little icing over the top of each puff. Let dry and serve in paper crinkle cups.

COCONUT MACAROONS

This is a simple, good macaroon. If you don't overbake, these will be nice and chewy.

1 cup egg whites	*1½ cups sugar*
(about 8 eggs)	*3 cups unsweetened coconut*
½ teaspoon salt	*2 teaspoons vanilla*

Preheat oven to 300°. Grease a cookie sheet. In a saucepan over medium heat, stir together the egg whites, salt and sugar until the mixture is warm. Remove from the heat. Blend in the coconut and vanilla.

Drop by teaspoonfuls onto the cookie sheet. Bake for about 20 minutes, or until golden brown.

While they are still hot, remove macaroons from the cookie sheet with a spatula. Place on a rack to cool. Serve in paper candy cups.

DATE-AND-APPLE SQUARES

These are very flavorful and will receive kudos!

CRUST:

4½ cups flour, sifted	4 egg yolks
½ teaspoon salt	4 tablespoons fresh
⅓ cup sugar	lemon juice
1 cup sweet butter,	2 tablespoons rum
chilled	⅔ cup sour cream

Grease a 15" x 11" x 1½" baking pan. Put the flour, salt and sugar in a large bowl. Add the butter cut in small pieces. Rub the mixture with your fingertips until crumbly. Add the yolks, juice, rum and sour cream by cutting them into the flour-and-butter mixture. Form a ball of dough. Knead for a few minutes. Wrap in a plastic bag and refrigerate for 1 hour.

Preheat oven to 425°. Using two thirds of the dough, roll to a rectangle a little larger than the bottom of the baking pan. Line the pan and press the dough against the sides of the pan. Bake for 15 minutes.

FILLING:

4 large apples, peeled,
   cored, thinly sliced
½ pound dates, pitted,
   chopped
½ cup pineapple wine
   (or a fruit liqueur)
4 tablespoons frozen
   orange juice,
   concentrated
Dash of salt
4 tablespoons fresh
   lemon juice

2 tablespoons lemon rind,
   grated
2 tablespoons orange rind,
   grated
1½ cups sugar
½ cup sweet butter
4 tablespoons cornstarch
4 tablespoons fresh orange
   juice

Combine the apples, dates, wine, concentrated orange juice, lemon juice and rinds.

In a large saucepan, cook the sugar and butter, stirring until the sugar is dissolved. Add the apple-and-date mixture. Cook for about 5 minutes, or until the apples are partially tender. Leave on low heat.

Dissolve the cornstarch in the fresh orange juice. Gradually stir this into the hot mixture, and when it becomes thick and glossy, remove it from the heat. Let cool.

Put the filling into the baked crust. Roll the remaining dough into a rectangle and use it to cover the filling.

Preheat oven to 325°. Before baking, apply the following topping:

3 tablespoons sweet
   butter, at room
   temperature
4 tablespoons sugar

1 tablespoon cinnamon
½ cup almonds,
   blanched, slivered

Spread the butter over the top crust. Mix the rest of the ingredients and sprinkle it over the buttered crust. Bake for 25 minutes.

When cool, cut into a little smaller than 2" squares to yield 4 dozen. Place in paper cups to serve.

DATE PINWHEELS

I recently invented these new cookies and my grandchildren were enthusiastic about them. The secret of success is the chilling of the dough and then the filled roll.

FILLING:

⅓ cup water
¼ cup sugar
2 tablespoons frozen
   concentrated orange
   juice

1 tablespoon rum
½ pound pitted dates,
   coarsely chopped
¼ pound pecans,
   finely chopped

Cook all the ingredients together for 10 minutes. Let cool.

COOKIE DOUGH:

½ cup sweet butter,
    at room temperature
1½ cups brown sugar
1 egg

1 tablespoon orange liqueur
2 cups flour
½ teaspoon baking powder
¼ teaspoon salt

Cream the butter. Beat in the sugar, egg and liqueur. Sift the dry ingredients and add to the mixture. Blend the dough thoroughly. Refrigerate for almost 1 hour.

On a floured board, roll the chilled dough into a 9″ x 20″ rectangle, ¼″ thick.

Spread the date filling over the dough, keeping it about an inch from the edges. If you spread it to the edge it will ooze out when rolled. Start rolling the dough from the long side, like a jelly roll. The roll will be about 1½″ in diameter.

Cut the roll in half. Wrap each half in wax paper. Chill thoroughly. You could also freeze for future use.

When ready to bake, preheat oven to 350° and grease a cookie sheet. Slice the dough into ¼″-thick cookies. Bake for about 8 minutes.

This recipe makes about 6 dozen cookies. Store in covered cans; it also freezes well.

FROZEN EGGNOG SHERBET

1 teaspoon plain gelatin

1 cup milk

3 eggs, separated

¾ cup sugar

1 teaspoon vanilla

1 teaspoon nutmeg

Dash of salt

½ cup brandy

1 cup heavy cream

Sprinkle the gelatin over the milk in a saucepan. Heat, stirring frequently, until the gelatin is dissolved. Cool.

Beat the egg yolks with ½ cup of the sugar until thick and light-yellow, then add the vanilla, nutmeg and salt. Slowly pour in the brandy. Stir in the milk mixture. Put in the freezer and leave it until the mixture becomes mushy.

Beat the egg whites to soft peaks; still beating, add the balance of the sugar to form a stiff meringue. Whip the cream to soft peaks. Fold the egg whites and cream into the semifrozen eggnog.

Return to freezer; let it stay until almost firm. Beat again. Freeze now until solid. Serve in sherbet glasses.

GERMAN LINZER SQUARES

1 cup sweet butter,
    at room temperature
1½ cups sugar
4 eggs
3 cups flour
1 teaspoon baking
    powder
½ teaspoon salt

2 teaspoons cinnamon
1 teaspoon ground cloves
2½ cups blanched
    almonds, toasted,
    ground
2 teaspoons vanilla
2 cups raspberry jam
2 teaspoons water

Preheat oven to 375°. Grease a 9″ x 13″ x 2½″ pan. In a large bowl, cream the butter, gradually add the sugar and 2 whole eggs plus 2 yolks (save the 2 egg whites). Sift together the dry ingredients and blend them into the batter. Stir in the nuts and vanilla.

Press two thirds of the dough evenly on the bottom and sides of the pan. Spread 1½ cups of the jam over the dough.

Roll the balance of the dough to ½″ thickness. Cut the dough into strips ½″ wide. Lay these strips over the jam-covered dough in a lattice pattern. Add water to the saved egg whites and mix. Brush on the strips of dough.

Bake for 30 minutes, or until golden brown. Remove from the oven and dot the remaining jam in each little opening of your lattice work. Let cookies cool in the pan.

With a sharp knife, cut into 1½″ squares. Place in paper candy cups to serve. Yields about 4 dozen squares.

🌹

COLD LEMON SOUFFLÉ

A very refreshing dessert after any kind of entrée.
Use 12 individual soufflé or custard dishes with a 2" foil collar tied around to give additional depth.

3 tablespoons plain gelatin	1 cup fresh lemon juice
¾ cup cold water	Grated rind of the lemons
2 cups sugar	Dash of salt
8 eggs, separated	1 quart heavy cream, whipped

Soak the gelatin in the water. In the top of a double boiler, blend 1 cup of the sugar with the egg yolks. Add the lemon juice. Cook and stir until thickened. Add the gelatin and blend well. Pour the yolk mixture into a large bowl and set it in a bed of ice cubes to chill. Beat until cool. Add the lemon rind.

Beat the egg whites and salt until foamy. Gradually add the remaining sugar, beating constantly until shiny and stiff. Whip the cream. Save a cup for garnishing, and fold the rest into the yolk mixture. Fold in the beaten whites. Taste for tartness. Add more lemon juice if desired.

Pour into prepared dishes and chill for several hours, or overnight. When ready to serve, remove the collars from the dishes. Using a pastry bag with a star tip, pipe the balance of the whipped cream around the edges of the soufflés.

I like to garnish my lemon soufflé with fresh mint leaves and cocktail maraschino cherries.

🌹

LIME PIE

This is an easily made, refreshing dessert.

Use 12 Almond Tart Shells (page 182).

FILLING:

1 6-ounce package
    lime gelatin
1 cup boiling water
4 ounces miniature
    marshmallows

1 quart vanilla ice cream
1 pint heavy cream, whipped
6 glazed cherries

Dissolve the gelatin in the boiling water. Add the marshmallows and stir until they are completely melted. Blend in the ice cream until the mixture is smooth. Fold in half of the whipped cream. Pour into the prepared tarts.

Put the remaining cream in a pastry bag with a star tip. Dot the whipped cream around the tarts; split the cherries and set them into the cream. Place the tarts in the freezer until well set.

These should be kept in the freezer. Move to the refrigerator 1 hour before serving time to get the right consistency.

STRAWBERRY OR RASPBERRY MILE-HIGH PIE

This is such a simple dessert, yet so satisfying.

Use 8 Almond Tart Shells (page 182).

FILLING:

2 egg whites
1 tablespoon fresh
   lemon juice
1 cup sugar

1 10-ounce package
   unsweetened frozen
   strawberries or raspberries
1 cup heavy cream

In a large bowl of an electric mixer, blend together the egg whites, lemon juice, sugar and frozen fruit (do not thaw). Beat at high speed for about 20 minutes, or until very thick. Whip the cream, fold into the filling.

Pour filling into cooled crust. Put in freezer until firm. A half-hour before serving, transfer from freezer to refrigerator for correct consistency for eating.

LEMON CUSTARD SQUARES

These come out with a layer of custard on top—a marvelous surprise.

1½ tablespoons sweet butter, at room temperature	3 tablespoons flour
	1 cup milk
	¼ cup fresh lemon juice
¾ cup sugar	½ teaspoon salt
3 eggs, separated	Powdered sugar for topping
3 teaspoons lemon rind, grated	

Preheat oven to 350°. Grease an 8″ x 8″ x 3″ square layer-cake pan. Cream the butter with ½ cup of the sugar. Beat in the egg yolks and lemon rind. Add the flour alternately with the milk and lemon juice.

Beat the egg whites with salt until foamy. Gradually beat in the balance of the sugar, a tablespoon at a time, until stiff. Carefully fold the whites into the batter and pour into the pan. Bake for 1 hour.

When cool, turn upside down and remove the pan. There will be a lemon custard layer on top. Sprinkle liberally with a shaker of powdered sugar. Cut into 2″ squares. Put in paper cups to serve.

MINT SURPRISE COOKIE

½ cup sweet butter,
  at room temperature
½ cup sugar
¼ cup brown sugar
2 eggs
1½ teaspoons water
1 teaspoon vanilla

1½ cups flour
½ teaspoon baking soda
½ teaspoon salt
24 thin chocolate-covered
  mint patties
48 pecan halves

Preheat oven to 375°. Grease or spray a cookie sheet. Cream the butter, gradually add the sugars, 1 egg, the water and vanilla. Sift together the flour, soda and salt. Blend the dry ingredients into the butter mixture. Chill the dough for 2 hours.

  Cut the mint patties in half. Enclose each piece of candy with a scant tablespoon of cookie dough. Place on the cookie sheet. Brush the cookies with slightly beaten egg. Top each cookie with a pecan half. Bake for 10 to 12 minutes until lightly browned. Let cool for a few minutes before removing from the sheet.

PECAN LOGS

These are easy to make and very tasty.

  Use commercial phyllo leaves, but after the package is unwrapped, keep the sheets covered with a damp cloth to make handling easy.

166

15 sheets of phyllo
  dough
1 cup sweet butter,
  melted

3 cups pecans, ground
½ cup sugar
2 tablespoons cinnamon

Preheat oven to 350°. Cut a sheet of phyllo in half crosswise. Use a half sheet for each log. Brush the phyllo with butter. Fold in half crosswise.

Combine the nuts, sugar and cinnamon. Put a tablespoon of the nut mixture on one end of the dough, an inch from the edge. Fold the end and sides over the filling and roll up into fingerlength logs. Repeat to get 30 logs.

Bake for about 15 minutes. Remove from the oven and brush each log with the hot syrup glaze. Let logs cool and dry.

GLAZE:

2 cups sugar
1½ cups water

2 tablespoons lemon juice

In a quart-size saucepan, combine all the ingredients, bring to a boil over low heat, stirring until the sugar dissolves. Brush the clinging crystals on the sides of the pan with a pastry brush dipped in cold water. Simmer the syrup for 20 minutes.

HAZELNUT PETITS FOURS

This recipe will give you delicious small cakes for elegant occasions—or to treat your family.

6 eggs, separated
½ teaspoon vinegar
1 cup sugar
2 cups hazelnuts, toasted,
  skinned and ground
½ cup crumbs, cake or
  graham cracker

1 teaspoon baking powder
½ teaspoon salt
Grated rind of 1 orange
2 teaspoons orange extract

Preheat oven to 350°. Grease or spray a 9″ x 9″ x 2″ baking sheet. Beat the egg whites until foamy. Add the vinegar. Gradually add ½ cup of the sugar, a tablespoon at a time. Keep beating constantly until you have a stiff meringue. Set aside.

In a large bowl, beat the yolks with the remaining sugar until the mixture is thick.

Combine the ground nuts with the crumbs, baking powder, salt and orange rind. Blend this into the yolk mixture.

Very carefully fold in the beaten whites, half the volume at a time, until they are no longer visible in the batter. Add the orange extract.

Pour the batter into the pan. Bake for about 25 minutes, or until the cake springs back when touched in the center.

Cool the cake. Cut into squares a little under 2″ each, to yield 25 pieces.

Ice the squares on the top and sides with chocolate butter frosting. Use a pastry bag with a star tube to decorate as you desire.

CHOCOLATE BUTTER FROSTING:

This, as you can see, is a very rich, extravagant frosting, that's also extravagantly delicious.

1 cup sweet butter,	*3 whole eggs*
* at room temperature*	*Dash of salt*
1 cup shortening	*1 teaspoon vanilla*
1 pound powdered sugar	*1 tablespoon instant coffee*
6 tablespoons Dutch	*4 tablespoons hot coffee*
* cocoa*	

In a large bowl, cream the butter and shortening. Blend in the sugar and cocoa. Add the eggs, one at a time. Add the salt and vanilla. Dissolve the instant coffee in the hot coffee and add to the frosting mixture. Blend well until the frosting is a good consistency for spreading.

This icing keeps very well, covered and refrigerated.

ORANGE PETITS FOURS

10 eggs, separated	*½ teaspoon salt*
½ teaspoon vinegar	*1 cup potato flour, or*
1½ cups sugar	* potato starch*
Grated rind of 1 orange	*2 tablespoons orange liqueur*

169

Preheat oven to 375°. Grease or spray a 14″ x 18″ x 1½″ pan. Beat the egg whites until foamy. Add the vinegar. Gradually beat in ¾ cup of the sugar, a tablespoon at a time, until the mixture is stiff. Set aside.

In a large bowl, beat the egg yolks until very thick. Blend in the remaining sugar, orange rind and salt. Beat in the potato flour. Very carefully fold in the beaten whites, half the volume at a time.

Pour the batter into the pan. Bake for 25 minutes, or until the cake springs back when touched in the center.

Remove the cake from the oven. Sprinkle the surface with the liqueur and let cool. Cut into 2″ squares. Ice with orange frosting. Decorate the cakes with the frosting put through a pastry tube to make it more attractive. Serve in paper crinkle cups for easy handling.

ORANGE FROSTING:

1 cup sweet butter, at room temperature	3 eggs ¼ cup concentrated
1 cup shortening	frozen orange juice
1 pound powdered sugar	2 tablespoons orange liqueur

Beat all the ingredients together until you have a good consistency for spreading. If the icing is too thick, add a little orange juice; if too thin, add a little more powdered sugar.

This frosting keeps well, covered and refrigerated.

SWISS FAVORITE

This is a unique cookie, chewy and rich.

FILLING:

2 cups sugar

1 cup heavy cream

2½ cups pecans, coarsely
    chopped, or blanched
    toasted almonds

In a heavy skillet on medium heat, stir the sugar with a wooden spoon until it melts completely and becomes a deep golden brown. If you're using a candy thermometer, it should read 320°.

All at one time, add the cream. The sugar will harden. Carefully stir until the mixture is smooth again. Remove from the heat.

Stir in the nuts. Let stand at room temperature for about 20 minutes.

COOKIE DOUGH:

1 cup sweet butter,
    at room temperature

½ cup sugar

2 eggs

2¾ cups flour

½ teaspoon salt

Grease a 9″ x 1½″ square pan. Cream the butter with the sugar. Beat in 1 egg plus 1 egg yolk, saving the egg white. Gradually blend in the flour and salt.

Press two thirds of the dough evenly on the bottom and sides of the pan. Spoon in the filling and refrigerate.

Preheat oven to 325°. Roll out the remaining dough between two pieces of waxed paper on a damp counter. Turn the dough onto the filled cookie pan. Dampen the edges and seal with tines of a fork dipped in flour. Prick the top. Brush the top with the beaten egg white.

Bake for about 1½ hours, or until medium-brown. Cool for about 10 minutes, loosen the cookie from the sides of the pan, but let cool in the pan.

Cut into 1″ squares and serve in paper candy cups.

THIMBLE COOKIES

A very simple butter cookie that is really good.

COOKIE DOUGH:

1 cup sweet butter,
   at room temperature
½ cup powdered sugar
4 egg yolks

2 cups flour
½ teaspoon salt
1 teaspoon vanilla

Preheat oven to 325°. Grease a cookie sheet. Cream the butter, add the sugar and egg yolks, one at a time, beating after each addition. Blend in the flour, salt and vanilla.

Form this dough into 1″ balls. Place 1½″ apart on the cookie sheet. Make an indentation in the center of each cookie with a floured thimble bottom. You can use your little finger if a thimble isn't handy.

Bake for 25 minutes. After baking, fill the center "hole" in the cookies with a little currant jelly or with chocolate filling:

CHOCOLATE FILLING:

Melt 4 ounces of semisweet chocolate with 2 tablespoons sweet butter and blend well.

STRUDEL

If you wish to make a genuine, pulled strudel dough, this is the method. You can then fill it with an apple, cherry or cheese mixture.

4 cups flour
2 cups warm water
4 tablespoons sweet
   butter, at room
   temperature

½ teaspoon salt

Grease a jelly-roll pan. With an electric beater, combine all the ingredients. Beat until thick but still quite sticky.

Put this dough on a clean counter or board and continue to beat with your hands. Don't add flour. Keep slapping and pulling the dough over and over again. The dough will become stiffer and rubbery. As you go through these movements the dough will begin to leave your hands. This process will take about ½ hour.

When the dough no longer sticks to your hands, cut it in half, making two balls. Knead a little flour into each piece. Place the balls of dough on a floured surface, spread the top of dough with a little warm butter. Cover the dough with a warm pan; let stand for 1 hour.

When you are ready to work with the dough, cover a table or large surface with a cloth. Lightly sprinkle flour on the cloth. Remove any rings to avoid tearing the dough, then dip your arms and hands in flour. Take a ball of dough, and on the backs of your hands start to stretch the dough. As you keep working with the dough over your hands and arms it will become too large to handle. Very carefully, transfer it onto the floured cloth. With floured hands, keep pulling the dough from all sides, using the backs of your hands from underneath the dough. It should be paper-thin. When completely pulled, use scissors to trim the thick edges remaining around the dough.

On the dough, sprinkle:

½ cup sweet butter, melted
1 cup cake or cookie crumbs

½ cup sugar and 2
*   tablespoons cinnamon,*
*   mixed*

Preheat oven to 375°. Now you can proceed to fill with one of the following (these fillings are for one piece of dough):

174

APPLE FILLING:

1 orange with rind
1 lemon, peeled
3 tablespoons orange
liqueur (optional)
8 large tart apples,
peeled, cored and diced
¾ cup sugar

Dash of salt
1 tablespoon vanilla
4 tablespoons sweet
butter, melted
¼ cup golden raisins
½ cup pecan pieces

Purée the orange, lemon and liqueur in a blender. Pour this over the apples. Add the sugar, salt, vanilla and butter and mix well. Sprinkle this mixture over the prepared dough. Now sprinkle with raisins and pecans. Fold over 2″ of dough all the way around. Lift the cloth and roll up the strudel.

Transfer the strudel from the cloth to the greased pan. Bake for about 45 minutes, or until golden brown. Sprinkle with powdered sugar. Cut pieces to desired size.

The strudel is best served warm. It freezes well and can be reheated to serve.

CHERRY FILLING:

2 #2 cans cherry pie
filling
4 tablespoons
Kirschwasser, cherry
brandy

½ cup blanched almonds,
toasted and slivered

Combine all the ingredients. Shape the filling into a log, right on the dough, about 6″ from the edge. Cover the filling with the 6″, now fold in 2″ of dough all the way around. Lift the cloth and roll up the strudel.

Transfer the strudel from the cloth to the greased pan. Bake for 45 minutes, or until golden brown. Sprinkle with powdered sugar. Cut pieces to desired size.

The strudel is best served warm. It freezes well and can be reheated to serve.

CHEESE FILLING:

1 pound farmer's cheese
   or ricotta
1 pound cream cheese,
   at room temperature
2 egg yolks
2 tablespoons cognac
1 tablespoon sweet
   butter, melted

3 tablespoons sour cream
½ cup sugar
1 tablespoon vanilla
¼ cup golden raisins
2 tablespoons cornstarch
Grated rind of 2 lemons

Combine all the ingredients and mix thoroughly. Shape the filling on the dough and proceed as with Cherry Filling.

INDIVIDUAL CHEESE STRUDELS

This is a favorite among my friends.

½ cup yellow raisins
4 tablespoons brandy
24 sheets phyllo
  (one package)
12 ounces farmer's
  cheese or ricotta
8 ounces cream cheese,
  at room temperature

1¼ cups sugar
3 egg yolks
½ teaspoon salt
1 cup sweet butter,
  melted and cooled
1 tablespoon cinnamon

Preheat oven to 375°. Soak the raisins in the brandy while preparing the rest of the ingredients.

Place the phyllo sheets between two dampened tea towels because they dry very quickly and become difficult to handle.

Prepare the filling by blending together the cheeses, ¾ cup of the sugar, egg yolks and salt. Add the raisins in brandy.

Place one sheet of phyllo on a cloth or lightly floured board and brush with melted butter. Fold the sheet in half lengthwise. Place 1 heaping tablespoonful of the cheese mixture at one end of the phyllo, 2" from the edge. Fold the small end over the cheese and then fold each long side over so the filling is covered. Brush the strip with butter, sprinkle with some of a mixture of the remaining ½ cup of sugar and the cinnamon.

Start at filling-end and roll up. Put the strudel seam side down on a jelly-roll pan.

Repeat the process with the other sheets of phyllo. Brush the strudels with butter and sprinkle with cinnamon sugar. Bake for 25 minutes, or until golden brown. Transfer the strudels to a rack to cool. Dust with powdered sugar if desired.

Serve warm, preferably. The strudels freeze well and can be reheated.

INDIVIDUAL APPLE STRUDELS

8 large apples, tart
Juice of 2 lemons
2 cups sugar
½ cup orange juice
½ cup almonds, blanched,
toasted and slivered or
chopped

24 phyllo sheets, place
between two dampened
tea towels
1 cup sweet butter,
melted and cooled
3 tablespoons cinnamon

Preheat oven to 375°. Peel, core and thinly slice the apples. Cover with the lemon juice.

In a large saucepan or deep skillet, combine 1 cup of the sugar and orange juice. Stir and bring to a boil over moderate heat. Wash any sugar crystals from the sides of the pan with a pastry brush dipped in cold water.

Add the apples and lemon juice. Coat them with the syrup and simmer for about 5 minutes, or until the apples are partially tender and syrup is reduced and thickened. Remove from the heat. Add the almonds. Let cool.

On a slightly floured cloth or board, put one sheet of phyllo. Brush with butter and fold in half lengthwise. Spread a heaping tablespoonful of the apple mixture at one end of the phyllo, 2" from the edge. Fold the small end over the apple filling, then fold each long side over so the filling is covered. Brush the strip with butter and sprinkle liberally with some of a mixture made of the remaining cup of sugar and the cinnamon. Start at filling-end and roll up. Put the strudel seam side down on a jelly-roll pan.

Repeat the process with the remaining sheets of phyllo. Brush the strudels with butter and sprinkle with cinnamon sugar.

Bake for 25 minutes, or until golden brown. Transfer the strudels to a rack to cool. Dust with powdered sugar if desired.

Serve warm if possible. The strudel freezes well and can be reheated.

ITALIAN PASTRY

This dough takes time to make properly. The results should be lovely, delicate, flaky pastries.

2 cups cake flour	2 cups all-purpose flour
(or all-purpose flour)	½ teaspoon salt
1 pound sweet butter,	3 eggs
at room temperature	½ cup white wine

Blend the cake flour with the butter. Form the mixture into a small rectangle. Wrap in foil and chill while you proceed with the dough.

Into a large bowl, sift the all-purpose flour and salt. Make a well in the flour and put in the eggs. Add the wine. With your hands, mix the dough until it is stiff. Should you need a bit more flour, add it carefully.

Place the dough on a floured board and knead until it is smooth. Using a rolling pin, roll the dough into a long rectangle.

Place the chilled butter mixture in the center of the dough. Fold the top third of the dough over the butter, and the lower third of dough over the upper fold. Now turn the rectangle of dough one-quarter turn clockwise. Repeat rolling and folding. Wrap the dough and refrigerate for 1 hour.

Each time you work on the dough, start by placing it another quarter turn right. Roll out, fold upper third down and lower third up. After rolling, folding and turning twice, once again refrigerate for 1 hour. In all you roll, fold and turn the dough six times. Chill after last turns. Prepare one of the fillings:

APRICOT FILLING:

8 ounces dried apricots
½ cup orange juice
½ cup sugar

½ cup cookie or
graham cracker crumbs

Soak the apricots in the juice for several hours. Add the sugar. Purée in a blender or food processor. Add enough of the crumbs to make a thick filling.

ALMOND FILLING:

½ pound blanched
almonds, toasted,
ground

½ cup cake or cookie crumbs
¼ cup raspberry jam

Mix the ground almonds and crumbs. Add enough jam to hold mixture together.

Preheat oven to 450°. Take the dough from the refrigerator and cut it in half. Put one half back in the refrigerator. Roll the one piece of dough to ½" thickness, cut into 2" squares.

Place a teaspoon of filling near one corner of the square. Moisten two edges of dough with cold water and fold dough over filling to form a triangle. Press the edges together. Place the triangles on a cookie sheet. Bake for 10 minutes. Then reduce the heat to 350° and bake until light-brown. Repeat this process with second half of dough.

To serve, sprinkle with powdered sugar.

CREAM-CHEESE TART SHELLS

This recipe will make about 60 tart shells when you use 2" muffin tins.

1 pound cream cheese	*4 cups flour*
1 pound sweet butter	*1 teaspoon salt*

Preheat oven to 375°. In a large bowl, blend together all the ingredients to form a soft dough. Taking small pieces of the dough, shape into balls the size of a large walnut. Put the balls on a tray, cover and refrigerate overnight.

In the morning, roll each ball into a flat patty and line the muffin tins. Bake for about 10 minutes, or until golden brown. Fill as desired. They freeze well.

ALMOND TART SHELLS

These tart shells are a little different from the usual. They are tasty and rich, yet not too fragile. They can be used for all sweet tart fillings and freeze well.

1/3 cup unblanched
   almonds, ground
2 1/2 cups flour
1/2 cup sugar

1/2 teaspoon salt
1 cup sweet butter, cold
1 egg, slightly beaten

Preheat oven to 325°. Use 2″ muffin tins. In a bowl, combine the ground almonds, flour, sugar and salt. Using your fingertips, rub in the butter until the mixture looks pebbly. With a spatula, cut in the egg until a ball is formed.

Take 1/2 tablespoon of dough and press it into each section of the muffin tins. Bake for about 25 minutes. This recipe should make 24 tart shells.

BLUEBERRY TART FILLING:

1 pint blueberries,
   frozen or fresh
3/4 cup sugar
Juice and rind of 1 lemon

1 teaspoon sweet butter
2 teaspoons cornstarch
1 cup heavy cream
1/2 teaspoon vanilla

In a saucepan over medium heat, place the blueberries. Add 1/2 cup of the sugar, juice and rind, butter and cornstarch. With a wooden spoon, stir until the mixture is thick and glossy. Cool.

182

Whip the cream with the remaining sugar and the vanilla.

Put a teaspoonful of blueberry mixture in each tart shell. Garnish with whipped cream. Refrigerate until ready to use.

CHERRY TART FILLING:

1 teaspoon almond
flavoring
1 2½-size can cherry-pie
filling

1 cup heavy cream
¼ cup sugar

Add the flavoring to the pie filling. Put a full teaspoon in each small tart shell.

Whip the cream with the sugar and put in a pastry bag with a star tube. Pipe on all the tarts.

CHEESE TART FILLING:

1 can (14 ounces)
sweetened condensed
milk
⅓ cup fresh lemon juice

8 ounces cream cheese,
at room temperature
1 cup heavy cream, whipped

In a bowl, beat the milk with the lemon juice. Gradually add the cream cheese and continue to beat until creamy. Fold in ½ cup whipped cream.

Fill 24 tarts. Put the balance of the whipped cream in a pastry bag with a small star tube. Garnish each tart.

LESS WICKED LEMON TART FILLING:

½ cup fresh lemon juice
1 can (14 ounces)
   sweetened condensed
   milk
5 egg whites

¼ teaspoon salt
½ teaspoon vinegar
2 tablespoons sugar
1 tablespoon lemon rind,
   grated

In a bowl, add the lemon juice to the condensed milk, stirring until thick.

Beat the egg whites until foamy. Add the salt, vinegar and sugar gradually, beating until stiff peaks are formed. Add the lemon rind. Fold the whites into the lemon mixture.

Fill 18 cold tart shells. Chill until ready to serve.

RASPBERRY EGGNOG TART FILLING:

1 tablespoon plain
   gelatin
½ cup sugar
Dash of salt
2 eggs, separated
1 cup milk
Dash of nutmeg

3 tablespoons rum
1 teaspoon brandy
1½ cups fresh (or
   unsweetened frozen)
   raspberries
1 cup heavy cream, whipped

In the top of a double boiler, mix the dry gelatin, ¼ cup of the sugar, and salt. Combine the egg yolks and milk, and add to the gelatin mixture. Stir over boiling water until the gelatin dissolves and the mixture thickens slightly. Remove from the heat.

Add the nutmeg, rum and brandy. Let chill, stirring occasionally until the mixture mounds slightly when dropped from a spoon. Fold 1 cup of the raspberries into the custard.

Beat the egg whites until foamy. Add the remaining sugar and beat until stiff. Fold into the custard. Blend in the whipped cream.

Fill 24 tart shells and garnish with the remaining raspberries. Chill for several hours, or until set.

CANDIES
&
FRUIT SWEETS

ROASTED ALMONDS

It is so nice to roast your own for the freshest-tasting salted nuts. You can use pecans, too, if you like.

2 cups whole blanched almonds

2 tablespoons butter
Salt

Preheat oven to 300°. Place the nuts and butter in a shallow pan in the oven for 20 minutes, or until almonds appear lightly browned. Shake the pan frequently during roasting.

Drain the nuts on paper towels. Sprinkle with salt and serve, or keep in an airtight container.

SUGARED ALMONDS

These are a fine confection. Toasting the nuts first is the secret of the special flavor.

1 pound shelled almonds
2 cups sugar
¾ cup water

½ teaspoon salt
1 tablespoon vanilla

Preheat oven to 350°. Place the almonds on a flat pan. Toast in the oven for 30 minutes.

In a 1-quart saucepan, stir the sugar with the water on medium heat until the sugar is dissolved. Wash the crystals from the sides of the pan with a pastry brush dipped in cold water.

Let syrup boil until a fork dipped in it spins a long thread, or to 238° on a candy thermometer. Remove from the heat. Blend in the vanilla and salt. Add the nuts, stirring quickly until they are coated with the syrup and the syrup returns to the white-sugar stage.

Put out on a flat pan to cool. Use forks or fingers to separate the nuts. These keep very well in cans.

ALMOND CARAMEL CHEWS

These are really delicious, keep well, and the effort exerted is worthwhile. Use a candy thermometer. All candies that contain cream must be stirred occasionally to prevent burning. To avoid graining, the candy should never be stirred more than necessary after it has been removed from the stove.

2 pounds sugar
2 pounds corn syrup
1 cup condensed milk
½ teaspoon salt
1 quart cream

2 tablespoons sweet butter
2 tablespoons vanilla
1 pound blanched almonds,
  toasted

Into a 3-quart saucepan, put the sugar, corn syrup, condensed milk, salt and one third of the cream. Stir over a low flame until the sugar is dissolved and cook to 236°. Blend in half of the remaining cream and cook to 240°. Blend in the butter and the rest of the cream. Cook to 244°.

Remove from the heat, add the vanilla. Pour the caramel onto a slightly oiled or sprayed marble slab or a 15"x 10" x 2" jelly-roll pan. Let cool. The length of time required for cooling depends on the room temperature. The caramel should never be cut until thoroughly cold and quite firm.

For cutting, use a strong, sharp bread knife. The caramel should be cut with a sawing movement. Never cut just bearing down. Cut the caramel into 2" squares.

Toast the almonds by spreading them on a cookie sheet. Place in a 350° oven and toast until they are golden brown.

For each square of caramel use about 5 almonds. Using your fingers, work the almonds into the caramel and form into a log. You will probably want to cut this log in two or three pieces. Then wrap each piece of candy in a pre-cut piece of wax paper. The paper should be about twice the length of the candy so you can twist at both ends.

This recipe will give you a large batch of chews. The candy keeps well in cans or refrigerated.

BRANDY BALLS

3 cups cookie crumbs
½ cup pecans, finely
   chopped
½ cup Dutch cocoa
½ cup brandy

3 tablespoons light
   corn syrup
2 cups powdered sugar
Dash of salt

191

Combine all the ingredients, using only 1 cup of the sugar. Form into walnut-size balls. Roll the balls in the remaining sugar. Refrigerate for several hours.

Put in paper candy cups. Yields about 3 dozen balls.

BUTTER NUT CRUNCH

*1⅓ cups almonds,
    blanched, coarsely
    chopped*
*1⅓ cups filberts, skinned,
    coarsely chopped*
2 cups sugar

1½ cups light corn syrup
⅔ cup water
¼ teaspoon salt
1 teaspoon cream of tartar
5 tablespoons butter

Preheat oven to 350°. Toast the nuts by baking them on a flat pan until lightly brown, usually for about 15 minutes.

In a large heavy skillet, combine the sugar, syrup, water, salt and cream of tartar. Cook over low heat, stirring constantly, until dissolved. Stop stirring. With a pastry brush dipped in cold water, wash the crystals clinging to the sides of the pan. Increase the heat to moderately high and cook the syrup until it is a rich amber color.

Stir in the nuts and butter. Blend well. Pour onto a large greased jelly-roll pan. Spread to about ⅓" thickness. Let cool completely.

Break into bite-size pieces. Store in airtight cans. Makes about 2 pounds.

LIQUORED FRUITS

Fill a plastic syringe with brandy and inject a few drops into fruits such as whole strawberries, soaked prunes, canned whole apricots or Bing cherries. Dip the berries in sugar before serving. Use these fruits as a garnish.

WARM FRUIT KABOBS

This makes a nice dessert, especially for the calorie-conscious.

2 navel oranges, peeled and cut in large sections	1 honeydew melon, scooped into balls
2 pink grapefruit, peeled and cut in large sections	1 small pineapple, scooped into balls
	1 jar spiced crabapples

Save all the juices you get while preparing the fruits. Set aside.

Using twelve 6" skewers, spear a crabapple on each skewer, then alternate other fruits. Place on a broiler pan.

SAUCE:

1 cup brown sugar	*½ teaspoon whole cloves*
½ cup water	*1 stick cinnamon*
2 tablespoons lime juice	*1 tablespoon sweet butter*

In a saucepan, combine all the ingredients except butter, plus all fruit juices you saved. Bring to a boil, stirring until clear and syrupy. Remove from the heat. Stir in the butter.

Pour the syrup over the skewers of fruits. Broil about 4" from the heat, turning and basting with the syrup. Serve warm.

DIPPED DRIED FIGS IN WHITE CHOCOLATE

These are attractive and so good.

4 ounces white chocolate	*Dried figs*
1 tablespoon vegetable	
oil	

In the top of a double boiler over simmering (not boiling) water, put the chocolate and oil. Stir until melted and smooth

Remove the mixture from the heat. Hold each fig at stem end and dip it about two thirds of the way. Let excess chocolate drain back into the pot. Place on aluminum foil to dry. Place dipped figs in paper cups to serve.

FROSTED GRAPES

I like to frost seedless grapes, but you can use malagas, or rebiers, for color variation. You can follow this same procedure with strawberries, cherries or other whole small fresh fruit.

2 egg whites	*1 cup granulated sugar*
2 tablespoons water	*1 pound grapes*

Lightly beat the egg whites and water. Pour the sugar into a shallow bowl.

Wash and dry clusters of grapes. Size of cluster will vary depending upon how you are going to use them. Dip each cluster in the egg whites, covering all surfaces. Let excess drain back into the bowl. Coat each cluster with sugar.

Set on aluminum foil to dry.

CHOCOLATE FRUIT BALLS

These are chewy and delightful!

*12 ounces sweet butter,
    at room temperature*
2 cups powdered sugar
½ teaspoon salt
*3 cups coconut,
    finely chopped*
*2 cups pecans,
    finely chopped*
*1⅓ cups candied
    pineapple, chopped*

*2 teaspoons instant
    espresso*
2 teaspoons hot coffee
2 teaspoons vanilla
2 teaspoons Kahlúa
8 ounces semisweet chocolate
*1 cup pecans, halved
    for trim*

In a large bowl, cream the butter and gradually add the sugar and salt. Blend in the coconut, chopped pecans and pineapple.

Dissolve the espresso in the coffee and add to the mixture with the vanilla and Kahlúa. Blend well. Chill for 1 hour.

Form into walnut-sized balls; place on a baking sheet.

Melt the chocolate in the top of a double boiler. Using a teaspoon, cover each ball with chocolate. Place a pecan half on top of each ball.

Refrigerate until set. Place in paper candy cups to serve.

QUICK DIPPING FONDANT

This is an easy-to-make fondant that can be used for dipping fresh cherries, grapes or other small fruits, fresh or dried, that you may want to cover for a decorative effect.

1½ cups sugar
¾ cup water
1½ tablespoons white
   corn syrup
6 cups powdered sugar,
   sifted

1 tablespoon cherry
   brandy (optional)
Few drops of food coloring,
   if desired

Combine the sugar, water and corn syrup in a saucepan. Stir over medium heat until dissolved. Wipe any sugar crystals from the sides of the pan with a pastry brush dipped in cold water, or a damp cloth. Cook the syrup for 10 minutes. Remove from the heat, let stand for 3 or 4 minutes, or until a candy thermometer registers 170°.

Start beating the syrup, and while beating, gradually add the powdered sugar. The fondant should be very smooth and still lukewarm. Add the brandy and coloring if desired. If the fondant is too thick, beat in a teaspoon of warm water. If too thin, add a little powdered sugar.

Dip the cherry or other fruit into the fondant, holding by the stem or use a small bamboo skewer. Drain excess fondant back into the pan. Let the dipped fruit harden on aluminum foil.

Note: The fondant may be covered and refrigerated for later use. Simply reheat and stir to dipping consistency over simmering water in the top of a double boiler.

SWEETMEAT TREAT

This is an uncooked confection. It is best when made a day or two before you intend to serve it. It mellows and improves in flavor. These will keep for 2 weeks without refrigeration.

½ pound pecans,
   finely ground
½ cup blanched
   almonds, toasted and
   chopped
8 ounces sweet chocolate,
   melted
1 egg

½ cup candied mixed
   fruits, finely chopped
⅓ cup raisins, chopped
¼ cup flaked coconut,
   chopped
1 cup sugar
¼ cup dark rum

In a large bowl, place the nuts, chocolate, egg, fruits, coconut and ½ cup of the sugar. Blend into a mass. Add enough rum to flavor.

Divide the mixture in two. Shape each piece into a long round log about 1½" in diameter. Roll each piece in the remaining sugar. Wrap in waxed paper and then in plastic.

When ready to serve, slice as desired. Put in large-size paper candy cups.

CANDIED GRAPEFRUIT, ORANGE AND LEMON PEELS

4 grapefruit   *8 lemons*
6 large navel oranges   *2½ cups sugar*

Cut the fruits into quarters, separate rind from fruit, keeping the rind intact.

Put all the rinds in a large saucepan. Cover with cold water. Bring to a boil. Pour off the water and cover again with cold water. Bring to a boil and repeat the process once more, bringing to a boil for the third time. Pour off the liquid.

When cool enough to handle, use a teaspoon to scrape all the white pith from the peels. Slice the peels into thin strips.

In a 2-quart saucepan, combine 1½ cups of sugar with an equal amount of water. Bring to a boil. Clean the crystals from the sides of the pan with a pastry brush dipped in cold water. Add the prepared peels and cook for about 45 minutes, or until the syrup has almost evaporated. Watch closely so that the peels don't scorch. Drain excess syrup from the peels.

Sprinkle a large tray or baking sheet with the remaining sugar. Add the peels. Mix and shake until the peels are coated with sugar.

Dry the peels on a wire rack. This will take a day in dry weather.

CHOCOLATE STRAWBERRIES

These are effective served as a plateful or in an assortment of other sweets.

For an eye catcher, buy a Styrofoam cone. Put a toothpick in the stem of each strawberry and push the other end of the pick at an angle into the cone. Cover the cone with berries in this manner and use the chocolate strawberry tree as a centerpiece for a tray of goodies.

4 ounces semisweet
   chocolate
1 tablespoon vegetable oil

30 large firm fresh
   strawberries with stems

In the top of a double boiler over simmering (not boiling) water, melt the chocolate and oil. Stir until smooth. Remove from the heat.

Hold the strawberry by its stem and dip quickly into the warm chocolate, immersing only two thirds of the way up. Let excess chocolate drip back into the pot. Place the fruit on aluminum foil to harden.

WATERMELON BASKET

A basket carved from a watermelon makes an attractive container for fruits on the buffet table. You can use your own creativity for a colorful assortment of fruits in season, cut to bite size.

Using a 10-pound watermelon, start the basket by cutting the handle: With a sharp knife, make two vertical cuts across the width, 3" apart in the top center of the melon. Go almost halfway down. Insert the knife at either end of the melon and cut horizontally as far as the center (handle) cut. Remove the two large wedges. Scoop out the edible melon from the inside of the handle, and hollow out the basket and the wedges. Cut the edges of the melon shell in a sawtooth pattern to make them more decorative.

Assemble your fruits. Make balls of the watermelon you have, and also from other melons. Wedges of fresh pineapple, raspberries, blueberries or strawberries, Bing cherries, clusters of grapes, orange and grapefruit sections, or slices of kiwi fruit. All can be artfully arranged in the basket.

I like to drape bunches of Frosted Grapes (page 195) over the sides of the basket. You can also garnish with dipped fruits, such as Chocolate Strawberries (page 199), Dipped Dried Figs in White Chocolate (page 194), glazed berries (dipped in Quick Dipping Fondant, page 197) or Liquored Fruits (page 193). Fresh mint leaves add a green touch.

For carrying out a particular color scheme, you can put a handsome ribbon bow on the handle of your fruit basket.

SPIRITED RAISINS

Use as a "nosh" or in a recipe calling for liquored fruit.

2 cups golden raisins	*Marnier, Kahlúa or any*
½ cup brandy, rum,	*favorite cordial or liqueur*
Cointreau, Grand	

Place the raisins in a sterilized jar. Very, very carefully, heat the liqueur *just* to the warm point. Pour over the raisins and seal the jar. Let stand 24 hours, shaking occasionally, before using.

When removing the raisins, strain the liqueur back into the jar. To replenish, add more raisins and more liqueur to the jar.

ROSE'S FUDGE

This makes a *lot* of fudge, which is what you seem to need as soon as one piece has been tasted. You can, though, cut the recipe in half.

8 cups sugar
½ pound Droste cocoa
8 cups whipping cream
2 tablespoons white
corn syrup

1 tablespoon vanilla
4 tablespoons sweet butter
Dash of salt

Sift the sugar and cocoa into a 12-quart pot. Add the cream. Put on a medium-high burner and stir constantly until the sugar is dissolved. It is very important to wipe the sides of the pan free of sugar crystals. Do this with a moist cloth or a pastry brush dipped in cold water. Repeat many times until the pan is free of any crystals.

When the mixture starts to boil, clean the sides of the pan again. Add the corn syrup. Let the mixture boil for about 3 hours over medium heat. Test a teaspoonful of the hot fudge in half a cup of cold water. If you can form a firm ball with your fingers, the fudge is done. If you use a candy thermometer, it should register 242°.

Pour the mixture into a large bowl, add the salt, vanilla and butter. Let cool undisturbed for ½ hour.

Beat the fudge until thick with an electric beater if you have one. Grease a large jelly-roll pan. Pour in the candy. With a spatula, smooth evenly in the pan. Let stand until solid. This could be 2 hours or more. Cut into desired-size pieces, using a sharp knife. Dip the knife in warm water between cuts if necessary.

🌹

NEVER-FAIL DIVINITY

Use a candy thermometer for these. It's a good investment if you are going to make these and other delights.

3 cups sugar	½ teaspoon white vinegar
¾ cup water	2 cups pecans, coarsely
¾ cup corn syrup	chopped
1 teaspoon salt	1 teaspoon vanilla
3 egg whites	

In a 2-quart saucepan, mix the sugar, water, syrup and salt. Cook rapidly to 240° on your candy thermometer. Be sure to wipe down any sugar crystals that form on the sides of the pan with a brush dipped in cold water. Do this several times during the cooking process.

Meanwhile, beat the egg whites until foamy. Add the vinegar and continue beating until stiff. Be sure that the syrup is still at 240°, then very carefully pour about one third of the hot syrup into the whites as you are beating them.

Keep beating the white mixture. Return the balance of the syrup to the stove and continue to boil to 250°, then pour it into the beating mixture.

As the candy becomes too stiff for the beater, remove and keep beating by hand until the mixture is creamy. Blend in the nuts and vanilla.

Drop the candy by teaspoonfuls onto a greased pan. Let stand until well cooled and set. Use a spoon to place pieces of divinity in paper candy cups. Dip your spoon in cold water if you're having a sticking problem.

MERINGUE MUSHROOMS

This confection makes an attractive garnish on a cookie or cake platter.

6 egg whites	*½ teaspoon cream of tartar*
½ teaspoon salt	*1 cup sugar*
½ teaspoon white vinegar	*1 teaspoon vanilla*

Preheat oven to 250°. Grease or spray 2 cookie sheets. Beat the egg whites until foamy, add the salt, vinegar and cream of tartar. Continue beating, and as the whites start to get stiff, begin adding the sugar, 1 tablespoon at a time. Add the vanilla. Continue to beat until you have a stiff mixture.

Fill a pastry bag that has a ½"-width plain tube: First make mushroom stems by pressing out small points on one cookie sheet. Make 40 or more.

Refill the pastry bag: On a second cookie sheet, make the mushroom caps by pressing out patties about the size of a half dollar. Don't make them flat! They should look like round pillows. Make 40 or more.

Put both filled cookie sheets in the oven for 1½ hours. Turn off the heat and let the cookie sheets remain in the oven for several hours.

Loosen the meringues with a spatula. Now you join the cap with the stem to form the mushroom by using a little frosting to hold them together.

CHOCOLATE ICING FOR THE MUSHROOMS:

*12 ounces semisweet
    chocolate
2 ounces sweet butter
2 tablespoons white
    corn syrup*

*1 teaspoon vanilla
1 teaspoon coffee liqueur
1 egg*

Melt the chocolate and butter. Add the syrup, flavorings and egg. Beat until smooth.

Spread the underside, or flat side, of the meringue cap with the chocolate icing. Now with the point of a knife make an indentation in the center of the iced cap to fit the stem. Insert the pointy side of the stem into the small hole. Let dry. If desired, you can sift a little cocoa over some of the caps to resemble brown mushrooms.

Pack in tins. Refrigerated, these will keep well for a couple of weeks.

SUGARED AND SPICED NUTS

*1 pound whole
    almonds, blanched
1 pound pecan halves
¼ teaspoon salt*

*4 egg whites
2 teaspoons cinnamon
2 cups sugar
½ pound sweet butter, melted*

Preheat oven to 350°. In a shallow baking pan, combine the nuts and salt. Roast the nuts for about 10 minutes, or until they are lightly toasted. Let them cool. Reduce heat to 325°.

Beat the egg whites until soft peaks are formed. Add the cinnamon to the sugar and gradually beat it into the egg whites. Continue to beat until the mixture is the consistency of a soft meringue.

Pour the butter over the nuts. Fold them into the meringue. Spread the combined mixture on the pan in which you toasted the nuts. Bake in 325° oven for ½ hour. Twice during this time, use a large spatula to turn the nuts over.

Let the nuts cool. Store in tightly covered jars or cans.

NOUGAT BASKET

This makes an attractive basket filled with small confections.

1 pound granulated sugar
Juice of ½ lemon

1¼ pounds blanched almonds, shelled, toasted, finely chopped

In a heavy saucepan over low heat, cook the sugar with the lemon juice, stirring constantly with a wooden spoon until the syrup is golden brown. Add the warm nuts. Blend well and spread on an oiled flat baking pan. Let harden slightly.

Now oil a shallow oval mold or a round pie pan. Cut a circle of the nougat large enough to line the bottom and sides of the mold or pan. Press it in firmly. (If the nougat becomes too firm to shape, place in a 250° oven to soften.)

With a pair of heavy shears, trim the edges and notch them decoratively. Let the nougat cool and harden. Turn it out of the mold.

With an oiled knife, cut a strip of the remaining warm nougat long enough to form a handle for the basket. Lay it over a small inverted oiled bowl to cool and harden. Dip the ends of the handle into caramel syrup and immediately affix the ends to the inside edges of the nougat basket.

CARAMEL SYRUP:

⅓ cup water	1 cup sugar

Combine the two ingredients in a saucepan and cook until the syrup is golden.

PECAN CREAMS

1 egg white	¾ cup powdered sugar,
Same volume of water	sifted
1 teaspoon vanilla	1 pound large pecan halves

Beat the egg white with water until it is thick and creamy. Add the vanilla. Gradually add the sifted sugar and stir the mixture until it forms a smooth paste, adding more sugar if necessary. Roll out a patty of the paste about the size of a quarter and sandwich it between 2 pecan halves.

Let the confections dry, then place in paper candy cups.

CARAMELIZED PECAN SQUARES

This confection takes patience to produce, but the result is worthwhile. Your friends will applaud you.

6 cups sugar	*½ cup sweet butter*
2 cups milk	*1 teaspoon vanilla*
¼ teaspoon baking soda	*6 cups shelled pecans*

To caramelize the sugar: In a large heavy skillet, melt 2 cups of the sugar over medium-low heat. Don't stir until the sugar begins to form a syrup (at least 10 minutes).

Reduce the heat from medium to low. Stir frequently with a wooden spoon until smooth and a light amber color, just a bit darker than honey. This takes about 20 minutes. It is very important that the sugar not get too dark!

Meanwhile, put the remaining sugar and the milk in a heavy saucepan. Cook over medium heat, stirring occasionally. When the sugar is dissolved, increase the heat and stir constantly until the mixture boils.

When the skillet of sugar is caramelized, pour it into the hot-milk mixture in a slow, steady stream. Continue to cook, stirring frequently to the firm-ball stage, or 244° to 248° on a candy thermometer. Remove from the heat.

Add the baking soda and stir vigorously as the mixture foams. Add the butter and stir until melted. Cool for 20 minutes. Add the vanilla and beat constantly until mixture stiffens and loses its glossy sheen, at least 15 minutes.

Blend the pecans into the mixture. Spread the candy on a greased 15" x 11" baking pan. When cool, cut into small squares and place in paper candy cups.

GLAZED PECAN HALVES

A candy thermometer helps, but is not a must.

½ cup water   Pinch of cream of tartar
1 cup sugar   1 pound pecan halves

In a small saucepan, bring the water, sugar and cream of tartar to a boil. Cook the mixture on moderately high heat. Wash down sugar crystals from the sides of the pan with a pastry brush dipped in cold water. Cook until the syrup reaches the hard-ball stage, when a drop in cold water becomes a firm ball, or to 250° on a candy thermometer. Remove from the heat.

With a pair of tongs, hold each pecan half and dip in the hot syrup. Place on lightly oiled sheet of waxed paper to set. Continue the process for all the nuts.

When cool, the nuts are ready to serve as a confection.

BREADS, COFFEE CAKES, & CRÊPES

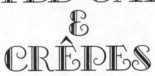

CHOUX PASTE

This is the dough that is used to make cream puffs or éclairs. It is also used for making dotlets or profiteroles, which are miniature-size puffs.

1 cup water
½ teaspoon salt
½ teaspoon sugar
   (eliminate sugar if not
   using puffs as a
   dessert)

½ cup butter
1 cup all-purpose flour
4 eggs

Preheat oven to 425°. Spray a cookie sheet with a nonstick product. In a saucepan, combine the water, salt, sugar and butter. Bring to a rolling boil. Stir in the flour all at once and beat vigorously until the mixture leaves the sides of the pan and forms a ball. Remove from the heat. By hand or with your mixer, continue to beat as you add the eggs, one at a time. The dough should be quite thick and have a satinlike sheen.

For an éclair shape, the dough should be put in a pastry bag with a large round tube. Press out fingerlengths onto the cookie sheet, leaving ample room for expansion during baking.

For cream puffs, press out mounds of dough or drop heaping tablespoons of dough onto the cookie sheet. Space well.

For the dotlets or profiteroles, drop dough by heaping teaspoonfuls onto the sheet or press small mounds through a pastry tube.

Bake in 425° oven for 15 minutes. Reduce the heat to 375° and finish baking for about 20 minutes longer, or until golden brown. Do not open oven while baking. After the shells are cool, cut off the top and save. Fill the bottom part, then return the saved top to cap.

This recipe will yield 12 large puffs or éclair shells, or it will yield 24 or more dotlets depending on the size desired.

PUFF PASTE

In France, a pastry chef thinks he has reached the ultimate in pastry baking when he has achieved a good puff paste. The dough is very delicate when correct and mostly used with custards, or flavored whipped creams in cream horns or napoleons. You can also use it for canapés, cutting baked pastry in small squares, and filling with a variety of appetizer mixtures.

1 pound sweet butter, *½ teaspoon salt*
  chilled *Juice of 1 lemon*
4 cups unbleached flour *1½ cups ice water*

Put the butter in a large bowl. With your fingertips, cream and squeeze the butter until all moisture is eliminated. When the butter is creamy, flour your hands and pat the butter into a 1½"-thick rectangle. Wrap it in a lightly floured sheet of aluminum foil and refrigerate.

In the same bowl, sift the flour and salt. Add the lemon juice to the ice water, and with your fingertips work the liquid into the flour. Keep working the dough until you can form a ball. Add a small amount of additional water if needed.

Put the dough on a floured surface. Knead it, pull it, stretch it and throw it hard against the surface until it is soft and pliable, not sticky. This process takes about 20 minutes. Wrap the dough in a large piece of foil. Refrigerate for ½ hour.

Now roll the dough to a large, thin rectangle. Place the chilled butter in the center of the dough. Fold the top third of dough over the butter, and bring the bottom third up over the top. Fold each side of the dough over this little bundle.

With a rolling pin, tap the dough gently. Start rolling the dough again into a large rectangle. Fold the top third to the center and the bottom third over the top, making three layers. Turn this piece of dough a quarter turn to the right.

Tap gently with the rolling pin and again roll into a rectangle and follow folding procedure. Make another quarter turn to the right. This is the second turn. Wrap and refrigerate for ½ hour.

Each time you refrigerate and remove the dough, you should have it in the same position as when you ended the previous process.

Remove the dough from the refrigerator, and tap it gently with the rolling pin. Roll, fold and make a quarter turn for the third time; tap, roll, fold and turn for the fourth time. Wrap and refrigerate for ½ hour or longer.

Repeat the above process for two more turns, or six in all. Wrap and return the dough to the refrigerator for several hours or overnight.

When ready to use, cut the dough in half. Keep the unused half refrigerated. Preheat oven to 425°.

Roll the dough as thin as possible. Place on a greased cookie sheet. Bake for 15 minutes. Reduce the heat to 350° and finish baking for about another ½ hour. When the dough is fully puffed and golden brown, remove it from the oven.

Set the oven up to 425° again. Roll out the other half of the dough. If you have 5" tin cones to make cream horns, cut the thinly rolled dough in 1" strips. Roll the dough over each cone, overlapping the dough until the cone is covered. Place on the cookie sheet to bake as above. When they are golden brown, remove them from the oven and carefully slide the horns off the tins, and let cool. They can be filled with sweetened and flavored whipped cream, powdered sugar sprinkled on top. Refrigerate until ready to serve.

With your first piece of baked pastry, you can make napoleon slices. With a sharp knife, cut the puff paste in 2" x 3" strips. Gently separate the puff paste into two layers. Spread each layer with a prepared custard or flavored cream, and top with another layer of puff pastry. Sprinkle with powdered sugar or decorate with whipped cream. Keep refrigerated until ready to serve.

Note: The unbaked dough freezes well, should you wish to use only half at a time.

ALMOND PASTRY CREAM

This makes a very fine filling for napoleon slices or in your favorite tart shell.

4 egg yolks	4 tablespoons sweet butter
1 whole egg	¼ cup rum
½ cup sugar	1 cup blanched almonds,
½ cup flour	toasted and ground
¼ teaspoon salt	1 cup heavy cream, whipped
1½ cups milk, scalded	

Beat the egg yolks plus a whole egg until thick. Add the sugar, flour and salt. Blend well. While beating, gradually pour in the hot milk.

Place the mixture in a double boiler. Stir constantly and cook until thick. Remove from the heat and place over ice water. Beat until cooled, adding the butter a little at a time. Fold in the rum, nuts and whipped cream.

Refrigerate until ready to use.

APRICOT DANISH CRESCENTS

This dough is tender, flaky, and delicious. The recipe makes about 75 pieces. They freeze well, or you can cut the recipe in half.

FILLING:

1 pound dry apricots
1 cup frozen
*   concentrated orange*
*   juice, undiluted*
1 cup sugar

½ cup water
4 tablespoons orange
*   liqueur*
½ cup cake or cookie
*   crumbs*

Combine all the ingredients except the crumbs. Let soak several hours or overnight. After soaking, purée in blender, small amounts at a time. Add the crumbs. Taste, and if too tart, add a little more sugar.

DOUGH:

1 pint heavy cream	6 tablespoons powdered sugar
4 tablespoons sour cream	2 teaspoons salt
3 ounces dry yeast	3 whole eggs
¼ cup warm water	3 egg yolks
2¾ pounds sweet butter	1 tablespoon rum
7 cups flour	

The day before you prepare the dough, let the heavy cream stand at room temperature overnight. Blend in the sour cream. This is called a *crème fraîche*.

Dissolve the yeast in the warm water. Set aside.

Put 2½ pounds of the butter in a bowl. Add 6 tablespoons of flour, and with your fingertips, work it into the butter. Form into a ball, then with floured hands flatten into a rectangle 1" thick. Sprinkle lightly with flour. Wrap in foil and refrigerate for at least 30 minutes.

Using the same bowl, sift in the flour, sugar and salt. Rub in the remaining soft butter. Blend in the eggs and egg yolks, flavoring, dissolved yeast and the *crème fraîche*.

Keep mixing until the dough is pliable. On a floured board, start kneading until the dough is smooth and elastic. Wrap in foil and refrigerate for 30 minutes.

Remove the dough from the refrigerator and roll it into a large ¼"-thick rectangle. Place the chilled butter in the center. Fold the top of the dough over the butter and the bottom of the dough over the top, making three layers. Bring each side to the center. Tap the entire package of dough with your rolling pin.

Start rolling from the center out toward the top, and from the center roll toward the bottom, making a rectangle. Fold the top third of the dough to the center and the bottom third over the top. Turn the dough, one quarter turn clockwise. This is one turn. Wrap in foil, place in the refrigerator without changing the position of the dough, for about 30 minutes.

Remove the dough from the refrigerator, and without changing the position, again roll into a large rectangle. Fold in thirds and make a second quarter turn. Roll out again, always rolling from the center up and from the center down. Do not use a back-and-forth rolling motion. Fold in thirds and make a third quarter turn. Wrap and refrigerate for 30 minutes. Repeat this process for the fourth and fifth turns. Wrap and refrigerate for 1 hour. Roll the dough once more. Fold and turn for the sixth time. Wrap and let rest in the refrigerator for several hours, or overnight.

When ready to use, cut the dough in half, leaving one half in the refrigerator. Preheat oven to 400°.

Roll the piece of dough to ⅛" thickness. Cut into 4" strips. Cut the strips into 4" squares. Cut each square diagonally.

Put 1 teaspoon of filling at long side of triangle and roll toward the point. Bend the ends to form crescent shape. Place on a greased cookie sheet. Allow space for dough to rise. Continue making crescents with all of the dough.

Let rise for about 40 minutes. Bake for about 30 minutes, or until golden brown. Bake only one sheet at a time. When cool, sprinkle crescent with powdered sugar.

BLUEBERRY MUFFINS

5 cups flour
4 cups fresh blueberries,
   or unsweetened frozen
1 teaspoon salt
1 tablespoon baking
   powder

1 cup sweet butter,
   at room temperature
1½ cups sugar
5 extra large eggs
2 cups sour cream
2 teaspoons baking soda

Preheat oven to 425°. Grease standard-size muffin tins. Sift the flour and put 1 cup of it over the blueberries. To the balance of the flour, add salt and baking powder.

In a large bowl, cream the butter and add the sugar and eggs, one at a time, beating after each egg. Gradually stir in the remaining flour and the sour cream, to which you have added the baking soda. Don't beat the muffin batter at this point, simply stir. Fold in the blueberries.

Put a heaping tablespoon of batter into each muffin cup. Bake at 425° for 20 minutes. Reduce the heat to 375° and bake until the muffins feel solid and are golden brown, for about 20 minutes more.

COCKTAIL-SIZE FRENCH BREAD

These loaves can be cut into thin slices for snacks and noshes.

3 ounces solid yeast	*16 cups unbleached flour*
1 cup warm water	*1½ tablespoons salt*
4 tablespoons sugar	*1 egg beaten with 1*
4 cups cold water	*tablespoon cold water*
8 tablespoons butter	

Preheat oven to 425°. Grease two 15″ x 10″ x 1″ jelly-roll pans. Sprinkle each with 2 tablespoons of cornmeal.

In a small bowl, dissolve the yeast in the warm water. Add 2 tablespoons of the sugar and set aside.

In a quart-size saucepan, put the cold water and the butter. Heat to lukewarm. Add the yeast mixture.

In a large bowl, sift the flour, salt and balance of the sugar. Blend in the liquid mixture. If you are using an electric mixer, stir at low speed until the dough leaves the sides of the bowl and a ball is formed.

Place on a slightly floured counter and knead gently for about 5 minutes. Cover and let rise for an hour. When the dough has doubled, punch it down and knead again. Let rise for another 40 minutes. Remove from the pan, punch down and cut into four pieces.

With floured hand, pat one piece of dough into a long rectangle ½″ thick. Fold one third of the dough lengthwise toward the center of the rectangle. Now roll up like a jelly roll. Transfer the loaf, seam side down, to the prepared pan. Continue in the same manner with the other three pieces of dough. Make five diagonal slits on top of each loaf. Let rise for about 30 minutes. Brush with the beaten-egg mixture.

In order to create steam for a crustier loaf of bread, put six cubes of ice in a tray at the bottom of the oven. Place the breads in the oven for 5 minutes, then put six more ice cubes at the bottom of the oven, reduce the heat to 400° and bake until golden brown, about 45 minutes.

COCKTAIL-SIZE RYE BREAD

The little extra effort required for this recipe will be rewarded by the results.

4 cups warm water	*4 cups unbleached flour*
3 ounces solid yeast	*1½ tablespoons salt*
4 tablespoons brown	*3 tablespoons caraway seeds*
sugar	*2 tablespoons coarse salt*
12 cups rye flour	*for topping*

Preheat oven to 400°. Grease a 16″ x 12″ x 2″ pan and sprinkle with 2 tablespoons of cornmeal.

Crumble the yeast in a saucepan of warm water. Sprinkle with 2 tablespoons of the sugar and set aside.

In a large bowl, sift the flours, salt and remaining sugar. Add the caraway seeds. Blend the dissolved yeast into the dry ingredients. Mix by hand until a ball has formed.

Remove to a lightly floured counter and knead until smooth. Lightly grease the top of the dough so it won't dry, and cover. Let rise for about 1 hour. Punch down and again knead until smooth. Cover and let rise again for about 1 hour.

Remove from the pan, punch down and cut into three pieces. With your hands, roll each piece into a long log, then place on the pan. Make five diagonal slits on top of each loaf. Let rise for about 30 minutes. Bake for about 20 minutes, then remove from the oven and glaze. Then bake for another 20 minutes, or until nicely browned. Glaze again and return to the oven for a minute or so. Remove from the oven and let cool on a rack.

GLAZE:

1½ tablespoons
   cornstarch

1 cup cold water
2 cups boiling water

Dissolve cornstarch in cold water. Add the mixture to the boiling water, stirring until thick and glossy.

When the bread is half baked, brush each loaf with this starch. Brush again just before removing from the oven. Sprinkle with coarse salt.

This will put a shine on your bread.

CRANBERRY FRUIT NUT BREAD

4 cups flour
2 cups sugar
1 tablespoon baking
   powder
1 teaspoon baking
   soda
1½ teaspoons salt
½ cup butter,
   at room temperature

1½ cups orange juice
2 extra large eggs, beaten
½ cup glazed orange
   peel, diced
1 cup pecans, chopped
2 cups cranberries,
   coarsely chopped

Preheat oven to 350°. Grease or spray two 9″ x 5″ x 3″ loaf pans. In a large bowl, sift together the dry ingredients. With your fingertips, rub in the butter.

Mix the orange juice and eggs. Cut the liquid into the dry ingredients, mixing just enough to moisten. Combine the fruits and nuts, fold into the batter. It will be very thick.

Pour the batter into the prepared pans. Bake for 1 hour, or until the center of the bread feels solid. When bread is cool, remove from the pans and wrap to keep moist. Slice before serving on buffet.

EGG TWIST, OR CHALLAH

The results of making your own rolls will excite you.

4 cups warm water
4 ounces fresh yeast
14 cups unbleached flour
⅔ cup sugar
1 heaping teaspoon salt
4 ounces sweet butter,
*   at room temperature*

6 whole eggs, plus 1 egg
*   for brushing*
4 tablespoons sesame
*   seeds or poppy seeds*

In a large bowl, put the warm water, yeast and ⅓ cup of the sugar. Stir and set aside.

In a mixer bowl, place the flour, remaining sugar and salt. Add the butter and 6 eggs and mix. Add the yeast mixture and beat on low speed until well blended.

Place the dough on a floured board and start kneading. Additional flour will be needed as you knead the dough. Don't put a lot of flour down at one time, just put a little as needed to keep the dough from being sticky. The more you knead, the finer the texture of the finished product.

When the dough no longer sticks, cover with a towel and let rise at room temperature. After an hour, punch dough down, knead again and then let rise, covered, for another hour.

Preheat oven to 400°. Roll a piece of about one fourth of your dough into a long log 2" in diameter. Cut into 1" pieces. You should get about 24 rolls.

Place rolls on a greased cookie sheet. Brush with the beaten egg and let rise for almost 30 minutes. Sprinkle with seeds if desired. Bake for about 25 minutes. You can use this dough to make a traditional challah or a simple loaf too. The challah is achieved by rolling the dough into strips and braiding.

SALT STICKS

1 pint milk, scalded and
   cooled to lukewarm
4 cakes fresh yeast
2 tablespoons sugar
6 cups flour
2 teaspoons salt

8 ounces sweet butter,
   at room temperature
4 tablespoons coarse salt
1 tablespoon caraway seeds
1 egg

Dissolve the yeast in warm milk and stir in the sugar.

Into a large bowl, sift the flour and salt. Stir in 4 ounces of the softened butter. Add the yeast mixture. Blend well.

Put a little flour on a board. Knead the dough until smooth and not sticky. Cover and let rise for 40 minutes.

Punch the dough down and knead again. You may have to use a little more flour. Cover and let rise again for 40 minutes.

Preheat oven to 400°. Grease a baking sheet. Divide the dough into thirds. Roll one third of the dough on the floured board until very thin. Spread part of the remaining butter over the dough.

Cut the dough into 4"-wide strips. Cut each strip into triangles. Roll each triangle from the wide edge to the point. Place the sticks on a greased baking sheet. Brush with the beaten egg and sprinkle with coarse salt and caraway seeds.

Repeat the process for the second piece of dough. Each third of dough yields 2 dozen sticks.

For variation, to make dinner rolls from the last piece of dough: Roll the dough into balls about the size of a walnut. Place into greased 2" muffin tins. Brush with egg. Sprinkle with poppy or sesame seeds if desired. Let rise for 15 minutes or so. Bake for 20 to 30 minutes, or until golden brown.

BASIC COFFEE CAKE

If you prefer a smaller amount, you can cut the recipe in half; however, the baked rolls freeze very well.

1 quart milk, scalded and
* cooled to lukewarm*
4 ounces fresh yeast
2 cups sugar
1 pint sour cream

1½ pounds sweet butter,
* at room temperature*
1 tablespoon salt
12 yolks, plus 3 whole eggs
16 cups unbleached flour

In a large saucepan, scald milk. When lukewarm, crumble in the yeast, 1 cup of the sugar and the sour cream. Set aside.

In the largest bowl of your electric mixer, on medium speed, cream the butter, add the remaining sugar, and the egg yolks, one at a time. Then add the whole eggs. Mix in the yeast mixture. Blend in 2 cups of flour at a time until the batter is too thick for the machine. Remove the dough to a floured counter and start kneading, adding a little flour at a time, as needed, until the dough feels smooth. Add additional flour carefully. You can always add more, but once you've added too much, the result will be a dry product.

Be patient. Just keep kneading and you'll see, as you work the dough, the texture changes and it gets thicker. When the dough is smooth and not sticky, sprinkle the counter with a little flour, place the dough in the center and spread with a little soft butter. Cover and let rise. This rising takes about 2 hours.

Now punch the dough and knead for about 5 minutes. Again spread a little soft butter on top, cover and let rise for about 1 hour. The dough is now ready to use as you prefer.

This amount of dough will make 2 dozen pecan rolls, 2 dozen cinnamon rolls and 2 dozen almond nut rolls—in all, 6 dozen rolls.

PECAN ROLLS

Use one third of dough from the original recipe for Basic Coffee Cake for 2 dozen large pecan rolls.

GLAZE (PREPARE THIS BEFORE ROLLING DOUGH):

¼ pound sweet butter
½ pound light-brown
sugar

3 tablespoons white
corn syrup
¾ pound pecan halves

In a saucepan, combine all the ingredients except the nuts. Cook over medium heat, stirring constantly, until the sugar is melted and the mixture is thick. This takes about 10 minutes.

Put a tablespoon of this syrup in each of 24 muffin cups. Put five or six pecan halves in each cup.

FOR ROLLS:

½ pound sweet butter,
melted
2 cups sugar

4 tablespoons cinnamon
¾ pound pecans

Cut the piece of dough in half. Roll on lightly floured surface to make a thin sheet. Spread with melted butter, sprinkle with cinnamon-sugar mixture and half the pecans.

Starting from the wide end, roll up tightly. Cut in 1½″ widths. Place, cut side down, in muffin cups.

Proceed in the same way with the second half of the dough. Let the rolls rise for about 1 hour.

Preheat oven to 350°, then bake for about 45 minutes, or until the bottom and top are brown. As soon as you remove the pan from the oven, put a flat pan or tray over it and turn upside down. Remove the muffin pans. Your rolls will be nicely glazed on top.

CINNAMON ROLLS

Use one third of dough from the original recipe for Basic Coffee Cake for 2 dozen large cinnamon rolls.

FOR ROLLS:

½ pound sweet butter,
  melted
2 cups sugar

4 tablespoons cinnamon
1 cup raisins (optional)

Spray two jelly-roll pans. Cut the piece of dough in half. Roll, on a lightly floured surface, to a thin sheet. Spread the dough with melted butter, sprinkle with liberal mount of cinnamon and sugar mixed, and raisins if you like.

Starting from the wide end, roll up in a tight roll. Cut in 1½" pieces. Lay the rolls in one of the pans, cut side up. Space rolls to allow for rising. Proceed in same way with the second half of the dough for your other pan. Let the rolls rise for about 1 hour.

Preheat oven to 350°, then bake for about 45 minutes, or until nicely browned. Ice while warm.

ICING:

4 tablespoons hot water
2 cups powdered sugar

2 teaspoons vanilla

Add the hot water gradually to the powdered sugar and vanilla, stirring just enough to give it a thick spreading consistency. Spread icing gently on hot rolls. Let them cool in the pan.

ALMOND NUT ROLLS

Use one third of the dough from the original recipe for Basic Coffee Cake for 2 dozen large almond rolls, or two long strips that you can slice.

FOR ROLLS:

*½ pound sweet butter,
  melted*

4 tablespoons cinnamon

2 cups sugar

*1 cup blanched almonds,
  toasted and ground*

2 tablespoons vanilla

Cut the piece of dough in half. Roll, on a lightly floured surface, to a thin sheet. Spread the dough with the butter, sprinkle with cinnamon and sugar mixed with the almonds and vanilla.

Roll the dough up tightly. Cut into 2″ slices and place on a sprayed cookie sheet. Space to allow rising.

Proceed in the same way with the second half of the dough, but instead of slices, let it remain in one strip. Divide the strip in half and place the two halves side by side in a sprayed 14″ x 10″ x 2″ baking pan. Let the rolls rise for 1 hour.

Bake for 45 to 60 minutes, or until golden brown. Sprinkle with powdered sugar when cool.

CHEESE BLINTZES

This recipe makes about 50 small blintzes. We like them best with sour cream and jam, or glazed berries.

CRÊPES:

6 eggs	*2 tablespoons melted butter*
1 cup milk	*½ teaspoon salt*
¾ cup flour	

Blend all ingredients in a large bowl. Beat just enough to combine—you want to avoid air bubbles. Strain the mixture to ensure smoothness.

The batter should be the consistency of heavy cream and the pancakes should be quite thin, but with enough body to hold the filling. Test one crêpe. If too thick, add a little more milk; if too thin, add a little flour.

In preparing the crêpes, I use two skillets to make them faster. Either spray or butter the skillets, then wipe with a paper towel. Heat until very warm, but not too hot.

Pour 2 tablespoons of batter into a crêpe pan. Rotate the batter to cover the bottom of the pan. Spill excess back into the bowl. Fry lightly, on one side only. Turn the crêpe out of the pan on a flat surface. The cooked side should be up. Continue until all the batter is used. The crêpes can overlap as you turn them out.

CHEESE FILLING:

1¼ pounds dry cottage
   cheese or ricotta
½ pound cream cheese
½ cup sour cream

½ teaspoon salt
1½ tablespoons sugar
3 egg yolks
2 tablespoons flour

Combine all the ingredients. Mix thoroughly. Taste for seasoning.

Place a scant tablespoon of the cheese filling in the center of each crêpe. Fold envelope fashion: from side to side, fold the crêpe over the cheese; fold the top side over the cheese; then roll to the other end like a little pillow. Place on a tray covered with a paper towel. Continue in the same manner until all the crêpes and filling are used.

If packaged carefully, the blintzes can be frozen.

To serve: Heat a large skillet with equal parts of butter and vegetable shortening for sautéing. On moderate heat, brown the blintzes, turning over only once.

If you want to fry ahead, place browned blintzes on a baking sheet. Keep uncovered in a 150° oven until ready to serve.

DELICIOUS!

BASIC CRÊPES

1 cup flour
*3 tablespoons sweet
  butter, melted*
4 eggs

2 tablespoons sugar
¼ teaspoon salt
1½ cups milk

Combine the flour, butter, eggs, sugar, salt and ½ cup milk. Beat with rotary beater until smooth. Blend in the remaining milk. Cover and refrigerate for about ½ hour.

Heat an 8″ skillet and wipe the hot surface with a bit of butter on a paper towel before making first crêpe only. Pour 2 tablespoons of batter into skillet. Rotate the pan quickly to cover bottom, spill off any excess.

When the crêpe is brown on one side, turn it over and brown the other side. Continue to make crêpes until all the batter is used. Yield: 12 crêpes.

STRAWBERRY CRÊPES

If fresh strawberries are in season:

*1 quart fresh
  strawberries, washed
  and hulled*

*½ cup light-brown
  sugar*

Slice the berries and toss with the sugar. Fill each crêpe and fold over. Sprinkle with powdered sugar.

If using frozen strawberries:

1 10-ounce bag whole
   frozen strawberries,
    unsweetened
½ cup sugar
2 tablespoons cornstarch

1½ tablespoons flour
½ cup water
Juice of 1 lemon
2 tablespoons grenadine
   (optional)

In a small saucepan on medium heat, combine half of the berries with the sugar, cornstarch, flour and water. Stir until the mixture has thickened.

Remove the sauce from the heat, carefully fold this cooked mixture into the rest of the frozen berries. Add the lemon juice, and grenadine juice if desired. Fill the crêpes and fold over. Sprinkle with powdered sugar.

LEMON MERINGUE CRÊPES

LEMON FILLING:

2 tablespoons cornstarch
1½ tablespoons flour
¾ cup sugar
Dash of salt
1 cup water

2 egg yolks, slightly beaten
¼ cup fresh lemon juice
2 teaspoons grated lemon peel
2 teaspoons sweet butter
½ cup heavy cream, whipped

In a saucepan on medium heat, combine the cornstarch, flour, sugar, salt and water. Stir until the mixture is smooth and thickened.

Remove from the heat. Quickly stir a little of the hot mixture into the egg yolks. Blend the warmed yolks into the cooked mixture and return to the heat. Cook for about 5 minutes, stirring constantly. Add the lemon juice, peel and butter.

Pour into a bowl and set over ice to cool quickly. Fold in the whipped cream.

MERINGUE & TOPPING:

2 egg whites
*¼ teaspoon white
vinegar*

¼ cup sugar
*8 tablespoons flaked
coconut*

In a small bowl, beat the egg whites at medium speed until foamy. Add the vinegar. Increase the beater to high speed and gradually add the sugar, beating until stiff.

To assemble crêpes: Preheat oven to 400°. Lightly butter a baking pan. Fill each crêpe with 2 tablespoons of lemon custard. Fold the crêpe over. Place the filled crêpes in the pan.

Pipe meringue over each crêpe, using a pastry bag with a small star tube. Sprinkle each crêpe with coconut. Bake for 8 to 10 minutes, or until the meringue is golden brown.

Serve warm. Yield: 8 servings.

CRÊPES SUZETTE

For a special occasion; this classic, elegant dessert can be made ahead and heated when ready to serve.

ORANGE BUTTER:

¾ cup sweet butter,
   at room temperature
½ cup sugar

⅓ cup Grand Marnier
   liqueur
¼ cup grated orange peel

With an electric beater, cream the butter. Add the sugar and beat until fluffy. Blend in the liqueur and orange peel. Set aside for spreading on crêpes.

ORANGE SAUCE:

½ cup sweet butter
¾ cup sugar
2 tablespoons orange
   peel, sliced in strips
⅔ cup orange juice

2 oranges, peeled and
   sectioned
¾ cup Grand Marnier
   liqueur

In a large skillet, melt the butter. Blend in the sugar, orange peel and orange juice. Cook over low heat stirring occasionally until peel is translucent. This takes about 20 minutes. Add the orange sections and ½ cup of the Grand

Marnier. When ready to use, transfer to chafing dish or electric skillet and warm on low heat.

Spread each crêpe with orange butter. Fold the crêpe in half and then in half again. Place the crêpes in the hot orange sauce. Gently heat the remaining Grand Marnier. Ignite with a match and pour over the crêpes.

MARMALADE CRÊPES

Instead of rolling the usual individual crêpes, stack these, and then cut the pile in wedges to serve.

¼ cup sweet butter
1½ cups sweet orange
  marmalade
⅓ cup Grand Marnier
  liqueur

1 cup pecans, finely
  chopped
¾ cup sour cream
  (optional)

Preheat oven to 300°. Use a shallow baking pan or ovenproof serving platter.

On low heat, melt the butter and add the marmalade. Stir until melted.

Working with 12 crêpes, prepare two stacks of 6 each. Brush a crêpe with Grand Marnier, then spread with the marmalade mixture. Sprinkle with a tablespoon of nuts. Add another crêpe and cover in the same manner. Place the stacks of crêpes in the oven to warm, for 5 to 10 minutes.

To serve: Cut the crêpes in wedges, pie fashion. A dab of sour cream on each wedge gives a nice contrast.

APPLE CUSTARD FILLED CRÊPES

This is an apple-filled crêpe baked in a custard with a caramelized topping.

APPLE FILLING:

2 pounds tart apples,
   peeled, cored, thinly
   sliced
½ cup orange juice
⅓ cup sugar

1 teaspoon lemon peel,
   grated
½ teaspoon cinnamon
1 teaspoon vanilla

Preheat oven to 350°. Grease a 10" x 15" x 3" baking pan. In a saucepan, bring to a boil the apples and orange juice, stirring constantly. Reduce the heat and simmer, covered, for 15 minutes, stirring occasionally. Blend in the sugar, peel, cinnamon and vanilla. Remove from the heat.

In the center of each crêpe, put about 3 tablespoons of the apple mixture. Roll up carefully and place seam side down in the pan.

CUSTARD:

2 cups milk
4 large eggs

½ cup sugar
½ teaspoon vanilla

Heat the milk and set aside. Beat together the eggs and sugar. While beating, slowly pour the hot milk over the egg mixture. Add the vanilla.

238

Pour this custard over the filled crêpes. Bake for about 30 minutes, or until a silver knife inserted comes out clean.

CARAMEL TOPPING:

½ cup sugar

Caramelize the sugar in a small skillet over medium heat. Cook the sugar until melted and golden brown. Drizzle it over the crêpes while warm.

BLUEBERRY-FILLED CRÊPES

½ cup sugar
2 tablespoons cornstarch
½ cup water
2 cups blueberries

1 tablespoon fresh lemon
  juice
1 cup sour cream
½ cup brown sugar

Lightly butter a shallow baking dish. In a saucepan combine the sugar and cornstarch. Stir in the water and ½ cup of the berries. Bring to a boil, stirring until thickened and translucent. Add the lemon juice and remaining berries. Simmer for 3 minutes.

Put some filling in the center of each crêpe and fold to enclose. Place the filled crêpes in the dish.

Before serving, spoon sour cream over each crêpe and sprinkle with brown sugar. Place under the broiler, six inches from the heat, until the sugar melts.

CHOCOLATE CRÊPES

FILLING:

½ cup sugar
2 tablespoons cornstarch
½ teaspoon salt
4 tablespoons Dutch cocoa

2 cups cream
4 egg yolks
1 tablespoon coffee-flavored
   liqueur

In a saucepan on medium heat, combine the sugar, cornstarch, salt, cocoa and cream. Cook, stirring constantly, until smooth and thick.

Beat yolks in a small bowl, add a few spoonfuls of the hot mixture to warm the yolks. Blend the yolks into the cooked mixture and cook for another 5 minutes. Add the flavoring.

MERINGUE TOPPING:

4 egg whites
¼ teaspoon white
   vinegar
Dash of salt

½ cup sugar
1 teaspoon vanilla
½ cup blanched almonds,
   slivered

Beat the whites until foamy. Add the vinegar and salt. Gradually beat in the sugar until the mixture is stiff. Blend in the vanilla.

To assemble the crêpes: Preheat oven to 350°. Lightly butter a baking pan.

In the center of each crêpe, put some chocolate filling and fold the crêpe to enclose. Place the crêpes in the pan. Use a pastry bag with a small star tube to pipe meringue on each crêpe. Sprinkle with almonds.

Bake for 8 to 10 minutes, or until the meringue is lightly browned. Use a spatula to remove the crêpes carefully onto serving plates or platter.

🌹

DESSERT CRÊPES WITH BEER

This beer-batter crêpe is another good basic one. If you don't need them all at one time, they can be frozen with *waxed paper* between each crêpe.

3 eggs
½ teaspoon salt
1 cup milk
1 cup beer, preferably
    stale beer

2 tablespoons sweet butter,
    melted
1 cup flour

Beat the eggs. Blend in the salt, milk, beer, butter and flour. Mix thoroughly. Cover the batter and let stand for 1 hour or more.

Heat a crêpe pan. Before making the first crêpe, put a bit of butter in the pan, and using a paper towel, grease the pan. You should not have to grease it again.

Put 2 tablespoons of batter in the pan. Tip the pan until it is covered with the batter. Pour off excess batter.

When the crêpe is golden brown on one side, turn it over and brown the other side. Stack the crêpes as you continue to use all the batter.

BANANA FLAMBÉ FILLING:

2 large bananas

Slice the bananas lengthwise in quarters and then crosswise in half. Place a piece on each crêpe and fold over.

SAUCE:

2 tablespoons butter

2 tablespoons brown sugar

1 tablespoon lemon juice

4 tablespoons rum

In a skillet, melt the butter. Add the sugar and juice. Cook to the caramelized stage, but watch carefully to avoid burning. Add 2 tablespoons of the rum and pour the sauce over the banana-filled crêpes.

In a very small utensil, carefully warm the rest of the rum. Ignite and pour over the crêpes.

CHEESE AND NUT FILLING:

2 tablespoons sweet butter

2 tablespoons sugar

4 tablespoons concentrated frozen orange juice

1 tablespoon lemon juice

6 ounces cream cheese, at room temperature

2 tablespoons sour cream

½ cup blanched almonds, slivered and toasted

2 tablespoons orange brandy

In a skillet, melt the butter. Mix in the sugar and juices. Cook for about 5 minutes.

In a bowl, combine the cream cheese, sour cream and nuts. Blend in a little of the cooked sauce. Place a tablespoonful of the cheese mixture on each crêpe and wrap them into small bundles. Pour the balance of the cooked sauce over the crêpes.

In a very small utensil, slightly heat the brandy. Carefully light it and pour over the crêpes.

HAWAIIAN FILLING:

*2 tablespoons sweet
    butter*
*2 tablespoons brown
    sugar*
*2 tablespoons
    concentrated frozen
    orange juice*

*2 cups fresh pineapple,
    finely diced*
¾ cup shredded coconut
2 tablespoons orange liqueur

In a skillet, melt the butter. Mix in the sugar and juices. Add the pineapple and coconut. Cover and cook for 5 minutes. Add the liqueur.

Fill each crêpe with a tablespoonful of the pineapple mixture and enclose. Place the crêpes on a serving platter.

TO FLAMBÉ THE CRÊPES:

3 tablespoons
   concentrated frozen
   orange juice

2 tablespoons sugar
3 tablespoons rum

In a small skillet, blend the orange juice with the sugar. Cook to dissolve the sugar. Add the rum. Carefully light this mixture and pour over the crêpes.

MY FAMILY'S FAVORITE PANCAKE

These are merely the best ever! Important note: Once you have the batter mixed, never beat it again.

6 eggs, separated
3 tablespoons sugar
4 tablespoons butter,
   melted
2 cups flour

1 teaspoon salt
2 teaspoons baking powder
2 cups sour cream
1 teaspoon baking soda

Preheat griddle to 375°. In a bowl, beat the egg yolks until they are thick or "ribboned." Gradually add 1 tablespoon of sugar and the melted butter.

Sift the dry ingredients. Add to the yolk mixture alternately with the sour cream, to which the baking soda has been added.

244

In a large bowl, beat the egg whites, add 2 tablespoons of sugar and beat until stiff. Fold them into the batter.

In making the pancakes, carefully take a large tablespoonful at a time from the bottom of the batter bowl. Place batter on the hot griddle. Cook on one side, then turn over once. Grease the grill for the first batch of pancakes only.

We usually serve these delicious pancakes with warmed maple syrup, Strawberry Hard Sauce or sour cream and strawberries, either fresh or cooked and glazed frozen berries. Serves 6.

STRAWBERRY HARD SAUCE:

½ cup sweet butter,
   at room temperature
2 cups powdered sugar

¼ cup brandy
1 cup strawberries

In a bowl, beat the butter until creamy. Beat in the sugar until fluffy. Add the brandy, 1 tablespoon at a time. Fold in the strawberries. Chill the sauce, covered, for 1 hour. Makes 2½ cups.

This is an excellent topping for waffles or pancakes.

THREE RECIPES EVERYBODY ASKS FOR

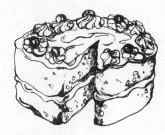

PECAN FUDGE CAKE

This cake was the most popular in our restaurant.

1 cup sweet butter,
   at room temperature
4 cups sugar
4 eggs, beaten
8 squares bitter
   chocolate, melted
4 cups pastry flour

4 teaspoons baking powder
½ teaspoon salt
3 cups milk
2 cups pecans,
   finely chopped
1 tablespoon vanilla

Preheat oven to 350°. Grease three 9″ layer-cake pans. In a large bowl, cream the butter, gradually add the sugar and beat until fluffy. Add the beaten eggs and melted chocolate. Sift the dry ingredients and blend in alternately with the milk. Add the nuts and vanilla.

Pour into prepared pans. Bake for 35 minutes, or until the center of the cake feels solid. Cool and remove the layers from the pans. Fill and frost.

PECAN FUDGE FROSTING:

½ pound butter
4 squares bitter chocolate
1½ pounds powdered
   sugar

2 teaspoons fresh lemon
   juice
2 teaspoons vanilla
2 cups pecans, chopped

Melt the butter and chocolate together. Blend in the rest of ingredients except the nuts. Beat well to spreading consistency. Add the pecans. Spread this frosting between the layers, and cover the top and sides of the cake.

To serve: Slice the cake with a sharp knife which you clean after each cut.

BLACK FOREST CAKE

This cake is featured all over Europe and, wherever I've gone in this country, publicizing *Grandma Rose's Book of Sinfully Delicious Cakes* (etc.), people ask for this recipe.

BATTER:

6 eggs

1 cup sugar

½ cup flour

½ cup cocoa

1 teaspoon baking
powder

½ teaspoon salt

10 tablespoons sweet
butter, melted

1 teaspoon vanilla

3 tablespoons Kirschwasser

Preheat oven to 350°. Grease two 9" layer-cake pans. In a large bowl, beat the eggs until thick. Gradually add the sugar, beating constantly.

Sift the flour, cocoa, baking powder and salt together. Carefully fold the dry ingredients into the egg mixture alternately with the melted butter. Add vanilla.

Pour into the pans and bake for about 25 minutes. The center of the cake should feel firm to the touch. While still warm, sprinkle Kirschwasser over the layers. Let set 10 minutes, then remove the layers from the pans to cool completely.

FILLING AND FROSTING:

1 pint heavy cream,
  whipped
1 tablespoon
  Kirschwasser
2 tablespoons sugar

1 #2 can cherry pie
  filling
12 glazed red cherries
1 bar or chunk of milk
  chocolate

To the whipped cream, add the Kirschwasser and sugar. Spread half of the cherry filling over one layer of cake. Cover with a thin layer of whipped-cream mixture.

Place the second layer of the cake on the first. Spread with the remaining cherry filling and cover with whipped-cream mixture. Ice the sides of the cake with a thin layer of the whipped cream.

Decorate around the top edge of the cake with rosettes of whipped cream. Put a glazed cherry in each rosette.

Make chocolate curls by shaving solid chocolate with a vegetable peeler. Sprinkle the chocolate on the top of the cake. Put a little chocolate on the sides of the cake if you wish.

BLACK FOREST TORTE

8 extra large eggs,
    separated
1 teaspoon cream of
    tartar
1 cup sugar
½ cup cake crumbs or
    cookie crumbs

1 cup blanched almonds,
    toasted and ground
¼ cup flour
⅓ cup Droste cocoa
½ teaspoon salt
1 teaspoon baking powder
3 tablespoons Kirschwasser

Preheat oven to 350°. Grease or spray two 9" layer-cake pans or three 8" pans.

Beat the yolks until thick, gradually adding ½ cup of the sugar. Blend in the crumbs and ground almonds. Sift the flour, cocoa, salt and baking powder. Blend thoroughly into the yolk mixture and add 1 tablespoon of the Kirschwasser.

Beat the whites until foamy. Add the cream of tartar and very gradually add the remaining sugar, 1 tablespoon at a time, beating until stiff. Carefully fold into the batter, a third at a time.

Pour into the pans. Bake for about 30 minutes, or until wooden skewer tested in center comes out clean.

After removing the pans from the oven, sprinkle each one with the remaining Kirschwasser. After 10 minutes, remove the cake from the pans.

FILLING AND TOPPING:

1 pint heavy cream
3 tablespoons sugar
1 tablespoon
Kirschwasser

1 #2½ can cherry pie
filling

If you prefer a dark cherry filling:

2 #2 cans black
cherries, pitted (drain
and save juice)

½ cup sugar
3 tablespoons cornstarch

Cook the cherry juice with the sugar and cornstarch, stirring until thickened and shiny. Cool and fold in the cherries.

12 glazed cherries
for garnish (optional)

Whip the cream until thick, add the sugar and Kirschwasser.

Place a layer of torte on a serving platter. Spread with a layer of the cherries. Cover with some whipped cream. Place the second layer of torte over the cream and repeat the cherry layer and whipped cream.

Put the remaining cream in a pastry bag with a star tip to decorate the top of the cake. Garnish with glazed cherries if you wish. (You do not usually ice the sides of this torte.)

INDEX

Eggnog
  Coffee, 127–28
  Heirloom, 127
  Orange, 126
  Raspberry Tart Filling, 184–85
  Sherbet, Frozen, 160
Egg Twist (Callah), 224–25
Escargot-Stuffed Mushrooms, 54

Farmers Chop Suey, 5–6
Figs, Dried, Dipped in White
  Chocolate, 194
Fish
  Gefillte Fish Balls, 59–61
  Kabobs, 55
  Platters, Lemon Basket Garnish
    for, 118
  Quenelles with Shrimp Sauce,
    56–59
  Sauce for Mousse, 70
  Stock, 60
  See also names of fish
Fondant, Quick, 197
Franks, Cocktail, 40
French Apple Squares, 135–37
"French Bouquet," 107–9
French Bread, Cocktail-Size, 220–
  221
French-Fried Shrimp, 83
French-Fried Vegetables, 7–8
Fried Cheese Balls, 99
Frosted Grapes, 195
Frozen Eggnog Sherbet, 160
Fruit Nut Bread, Cranberry, 223–
  224
Fruit Sweets, see Candies
Fudge, Rose's, 202–3
Fudge Pecan Cake, 249–50

Garnish Suggestions, 116–19
Gefillte Fish Balls, 59–61
German Linzer Squares, 161
Glazed Pecan Halves, 209
Glazed Shrimp, 82
Grapefruit Peels, Candied, 199
Grapes, Frosted, 195
Great Spear-It Combinations, 36–
  37
Green Peppers, Chinese-Style
  Beef with, 37–38

Ham
  -Filled Mushroom Caps, 38–39
  Kabobs, 39
  Pineapple Stuffed Eggs, 96
  Rolls, Toasted, 122
Hawaiian Filling for Crêpes, 243

Hazelnut Petits Fours, 168–69
Heirloom Eggnog, 127
Herring, 61–64
  Chopped Salad, 62–63
  Ring Filled with Shrimp, 63–64
  in Sour Cream, 62
  -Stuffed Beets, 61
Hors d'Oeuvres, 93–125
  Anchovy Canapé, 121
  Anchovy Dip, 123
  Artichoke Canapé, 122–23
  Assorted Cheese Platter, 100–1
  Assorted Cold Cuts and Cheese
    Platter, 111–12
  Avocado Tomato Dip, 124
  Beet-and-Prune Relish, 112
  Caviar Towers, 119–20
  Cheese-Puff Squares, 101–4
  Cream-Cheese Pastry Shells,
    105–7
  Deviled-Egg Shrimp Basket, 97
  Egg Basket with Caviar, 98
  Fried Cheese Balls, 99
  Garnish Suggestions, 116–19
  Hot Chili Dip, 124–25
  Macadamia Cheese Balls, 98–
    99
  My "French Bouquet," 107–9
  My Special Mustard, 109
  Old-Fashioned Buffet Supper,
    110–11
  Pheasant Pie, 112–14
  Pineapple Ham Stuffed Eggs,
    96
  Quick Pick-ups, 114–15
  Ravigote Sauce, 110
  Reuben Sandwich, 115–16
  Salmon-Stuffed Eggs, 95–96
  Sautéed Livers with Apple, 120
  Shrimp Dip, 123
  Smoked Salmon and Cucumber
    Dip, 125
  Stuffed Eggs, 95
  Tartlets, 104–5
  Toasted Ham Rolls, 122
  Waffled Beef and Cheese, 121
Horseradish Ring Filled with
  Shrimp Salad, 80–81
Hot Chili Dip, 124–25

Individual Apple Strudels, 178–79
Individual Cheese Strudels, 177–
  178
Italian Pastry, 179–81

Kabobs
  Fish, 55

Ham, 39
  Warm Fruit, 193–94

Lemon
  Basket, Garnish for Fish
    Platters, 118
  Chicken, Oriental, 29–30
  Custard Squares, 165
  Meringue Crêpes, 234–35
  Peels, Candied, 199
  Soufflé, Cold, 162
  Tart Filling, 184
Lime
  Pie, 163
  Scallops with, 74–75
Liquored Fruits, 193
Lox Roulades (Smoked Salmon),
  71

Macadamia Cheese Balls, 98–99
Macaroons, Coconut, 155
Marinated Mushroom Caps, 8
Marmalade Crêpes, 237
Mayonnaise, 33
Meat, 34–40
  Beef Tenderloin and Mushroom
    en Brochette, 35–36
  Chinese-Style Beef with Green
    Peppers, 37–38
  Cocktail Franks, 40
  Great Spear-It Combinations,
    36–37
  Ham Kabobs, 39
  Ham-Filled Mushroom Caps,
    38–39
  Spicy Small Burgers, 34–35
Meringue
  Chocolate, Relatively Low-
    Calorie, 152
  Floats for Orange Eggnog, 126
  Lemon Crêpes, 234–35
  Mushrooms, 204–5
  Topping for Brownies, 141
  Topping for Crêpes, 235, 240
Mint Surprise Cookie, 166
Mousse
  Crab-and-Shrimp, 53
  Puffs, Chocolate, 153–55
  Red-Caviar, 43–44
  Salmon-and-Sturgeon, 69–70
Muffins, Blueberry, 220
Mushroom(s)
  and Beef Tenderloin en
    Brochette, 35–36
  Caps, Marinated, 8
  Chicken Livers with, 31–32
  Escargot-Stuffed, 54

ABOUT THE AUTHOR

Born in Russia, ROSE NAFTALIN began commercial baking during the Depression when she and her husband opened a little delicatessen in Toledo, Ohio. She later settled in Portland, Oregon, where her restaurant "Rose's" became famous throughout the country for the gargantuan size and superlative quality of her baked goods. Her first book, Grandma Rose's Book of Sinfully Delicious Cakes, Cookies, Pies, Cheese Cakes, Cake Rolls & Pastries *was excerpted in* Family Circle *and was a book-club selection of the Better Homes & Gardens Book Club, the Family Book Service and the Cookbook Guild.*

She now lives in Portland, where the smells from her kitchen draw her lucky children, grandchildren and great-grandchildren to her door.